BEYOND
EMOTIONAL
INTELLIGENCE

URM
education
SILICON VALLEY

RICHARD LOUIS MATTHEWS

BEYOND EMOTIONAL INTELLIGENCE

A whole brain approach to teaching,
learning and management

7th Edition – International Release

URM
education
SILICON VALLEY

License Copyright © 2021 URM Education LLC.

Original Title: Além da Inteligência Emocional © 1997
7th Edition – International Release

Publisher: **URM Education LLC - 2021**

Author's pseudonym: **Richard Louis Matthews**

Published in the United States in hardcover by URM Education LLC, Silicon Valley, California.

This book is available for bulk purchases for corporate use. Special editions, including personalized covers, or books with corporate logos can be created in large quantities for special needs. For more information, contact URM Education team at info@urmeducation.com

Cataloging in Publication (CIP)
(Librarian - Maria Helena Ferreira Xavier da Silva CRB7-5688)

Library of Congress Cataloging-in-Publication Data
Matthews, Richard Louis, 1980
  Beyond Emotional Intelligence / Richard Louis Matthews – 7th ed.
    p. cm.
1. Business administration.   2. Leadership   3. Organizational Behavior.
I. Title.

ISBN: 978-1-66780-955-7

Printed in United States of America

Book design by Henrique Albiero Miranda
Cover and Jacket design by Julio Rodrigues (Casulo)

Seventh Edition   CDD 152.4

Summary

All sciences, arts, disciplines
and subsidiary technologies
were originally generated by the skills
of the oldest and sophisticated device
made available to men: his brain.
Sciences, technologies and disciplines
can only solve sectoral problems.
Intelligence is the only universal panacea.

Multiple Intelligences

As a consequence of its age-old evolutionary process, the human brain houses dozens of specific "intelligence centers".

It is not difficult to understand this.

The most remote ancestors of man, great-grandparents of prehistoric reptiles, had a very limited brain system, with skills essential to the provision of their survival.

They have exercised these primary skills over millennia, and have certainly become very efficient in their management.

The same happened with their descendants, passing through the first mammals until reaching the closest relatives of man.

Each of these species, as their brain skills slowly developed, generation after generation, had the opportunity to make extensive use of these skills.

By reconstituting the brain's evolutionary process, from reptiles to contemporary man, science summarized the skills that developed sequentially into three major groups or levels of skills (Figure I.1).

1. Medullary
2. Lower Brain (cortical)
3. Upper Brain (neocortical)

The first two levels, identified as the reptilian brain (or lizard brain), comprise what science has called the limbic system of the human brain, responsible for unconscious and subconscious organic activities and for all man's instinctual-emotional reactions.

The upper cerebral level or neocortical system (from cortex, cork or cover) is responsible for all the intellectual elaborations and deliberate actions of man.

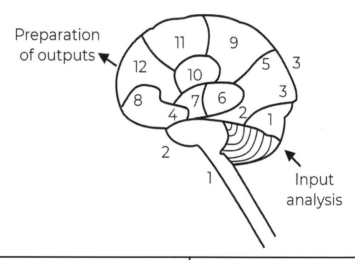

Figure 1.1. Scientific Information

1. Medulla
   Walking & Corporal reflexes
 	
2. Cerebellum
   Sub conscient
   organic activities
	3. Cerebral Cortex
	1. Vision
	2. Names of objects
	3. Visual words processing
	4. Emotions
	5. Space coordination and body context
	6. Language comprehension
	7. Auditory
	8. Behavior
	9. Sensorial
	10. Word Processing
	11. Motrix
	12. Complex movements and elaboration of thoughts

At the same time, intellectual skills do not have sofar the exhaustive "training" of limbic skills nor, consequently, the ability to deliver to man his full potential. The possibility or the dream that the human being can access, use and fully develop his aptitudes has been the target of diverse proposals, such as the one related to the left and right cerebral hemispheres (cerebral duality), developing to the cerebral quadrants, to transactional analysis, to neurolinguistic programming (NLP) and, more recently, to "emotional intelligence" (Daniel Goleman, October 1995).

In the book Mastering the Powers of the Mind, edited 1995, I have explained in detail the process of development of the cerebral aptitudes of the human being throughout the various stages of evolution of the species, building the concept of cerebral multipolarity, which clarifies and harmonizes, in a single version, all concepts explored in brain duality and Ned Hermann's quadrality, in the "seven types of intelligence" proposed by Howard Gardner, in the theories of behavior from Maslow's hierarchy of human needs, through transactional analysis and neurolinguistic programming to parapsychological and spiritual phenomena.

This concept explained step by step from page 23 to 32, allows us to understand how the skills found today in the human brain developed, from the lower brain system, present in reptiles, to the cortical system of mammals, reaching the neo-cortical complex of man.

In this three-layered brain, the two oldest, the lower portions of it, harbor all the operational or emotional skills, while the purely intellectual skills of the human brain dwells the upper new cortex domain, which we have become accustomed to specifically call intelligence.

However, the concept of cerebral duality, proposed more than 40 years ago, already suggested two types of "intelligence" – a "quantitative" and a "qualitative" and, in the last decade, the concepts of "multiple intelligences" began to proliferate highlighted in the work of Howard Gardner, master of education at Harvard.

Upon learning of Goleman's work on emotional intelligence, we found that the concept of cerebral multipolarity provides full coverage and facilitates a clear understanding of the approaches proposed by emotional intelligence, allowing the assessment and appropriation of each individual's intellectual and emotional potential.

* * *

This book is an enlarged and enriched edition of the original 1995 work (Mastering the Powers of Mind /Beyond Neurolinguistics) including roadmaps, proposals and procedures for access, control, development and full use of all brain skills in the processes of teaching and learning, communication and negotiation, approach and creative problem solving, teamwork, leadership and business management.

Under these conditions, it becomes a work of extraordinary value in all human activities, as a source of consultation, guidance and exercises for the personal and professional development of the reader.

We wish you a happy journey throughout these pages.

1

The three layer Brain

Some of the most remote ancestors of man, such as the reptiles of the Teriodon family, living in the Triassic and Jurassic, more than 200 million years ago, had a brain no larger than an egg, although they could reach 25 meters in length and 35 tons of weight.

Their brain's capacity was limited to promoting the essential movements to their survival and subsistence, represented by the actions of eating and procreating.

To eat and procreate, the first inhabitants of the planet, remote ancestors of the Teriodon, needed nothing more than appetite. The Teriodon had already learned to fight for food with all his competitors, to dispute females with his peers and, also, to guarantee his survival through association with other animals of his species, living in flocks.

Action, reaction and escape, coexistence and grouping were the essential skills of the "lizard brain" that persist, even today, as the fundamental skills of the central nervous system of most of all known animals, including mammals and man.

While recognizing the paradox of the brain being the most important and least known of Organs component of the human body, science has already managed to catalog a lot of information about its physiology and functioning.

Of this information, the most important for understanding the problem related to the development of brain aptitude refer, first of all, the clear definition that the functions that we usually attribute to the "brain" are, in reality, performed by a set of organisms. In command of the entire nervous system including the medulla, cerebellum and cerebral cortex, in addition to several intermediate organs: bulb, bridge, thalamus and amygdala, highlighted.

Second, there is the perception that the structure of this system, in all animals, have peculiar characteristics derived from a primitive model – the brain of prehistoric reptiles, similar to the one of the lizards of our time, which underwent subsequent evolutions. over the centuries and millennia, providing the perception that this system continues to evolve.

Science recognizes that the human central nervous system has characteristics acquired at each stage of evolutionary development and that, from this heritage, it is possible to identify three main levels of specific functional attributes:

The medullary level, primarily responsible for gait movements, reflexes to move away parts of the body from threatening objects, lower limbs stretching to support the body's weight, reflexes that control blood vessels, gastrointestinal movements and other.

The lower brain level, responsible for much, if not most, of subconscious organic activities: blood pressure and breathing, balance eating control reflexes (salivation, licking the lips) and emotional responses such as anger, excitement, sex, reaction to pain and pleasure.

The upper brain level, responsible for storing

information, for the intellectual elaborations that give rise to deliberate movements and for supporting the functions and operations of the lower brain centers, to which it lends precision.

Science has also managed to establish that the cerebral cortex never works alone, but always in association with the lower brain centers that maintain the cerebral cortex on alert, opening its "database" to the brain's thinking machine.

It is easy to see that the cerebral cortex has basically conceptual attributions, leaving to the "limbic system" – the association of the oldest parts of the brain – the responsability for most of the motor and functional activities of the brain.

In other words, the cerebral cortex mainly thinks, while the limbic system mainly moves actions and reactions.

Scientific research also reported that the different functions of the cerebral cortex and the neocortex – the intellectual functions of the brain, occupy specific positions throughout the brain mass.

Looking closely at the position of these functions (page 8), we will notice that they are distributed along a sequence from dorsal to frontal and inferior to superior, in which the centers of perception and interpretation of stimuli coming from the environment are located in the lower and posterior regions of the brain, while the centers for elaborating responses to the environment are located in the highest and para-frontal regions of the cortex.

Figure 1.1, extracted from the Theaty on Medical Physiology, by Arthur C. Guyton, textbook of medical schools, from which the scientific information focused up to this point has been transcribed, clearly suggest this direction of development.

In this figure, the notes "Input analysis" and "Preparation of outputs" are not included in the quoted Guyton´s original information, being suggested by us.

Scientific information allows us to understand that the evolution of the brain Figure 1.2), over millennia, started with a "small brain" (cerebellum) passing through a larger brain with greater skills, present in all mammals, evolving sequentially to the contemporary human brain and, certainly, in a continuous process of evolution towards the super brain of the man of the future.

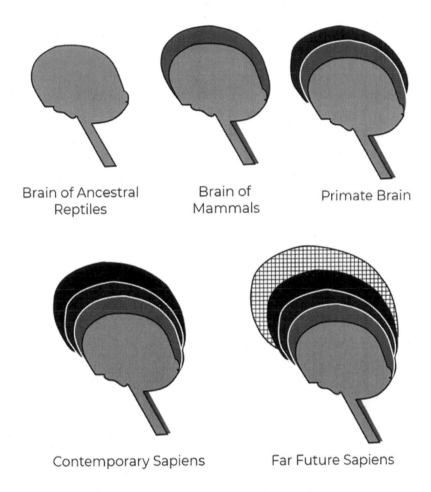

Brain of Ancestral
Reptiles

Brain of
Mammals

Primate Brain

Contemporary Sapiens

Far Future Sapiens

Figure1.2 Brain evolution throughout millennia

New born   Baby

Todler   Young and Adult

Figure 1.3 Sequential occupation of brain skills

In view of this observation, it is curious to percieve that the installation of this brain capacity, which required millennia of evolution, is reproduced in a few months and years in the process of appropriation of these capacities by modern man.

At birth, man has only the skills listed in the first stage of the evolution of species under his control.

Although the newborn already brings a brain with all the skills listed at the three levels described, he is only able to use the limbic skills essential to sustaining his life at a stage as primary as crying and sipping the food placed in his mouth.

All lower animals on the zoological scale are, at birth, much more apt than man.

However, in a few days and months, the human being is mastering the abilities that make him a superior and unique animal.

If you follow, step by step, the development of the human embryo, you will have a glimpse of the evolutionary process, from a small fish with gills and a tail that it will lose to be born almost identical to a baby monkey.

Playing a quick movie of the first months of a child's life, you would see him crawling and walking on all fours until the most decisive moment of his evolution, when he stands on his hind legs.

You would have just missed a moment much more decisive than that. The moment when he cames out of the water, minutes before giving birth.

At eight years of age, any child already has all the skills he will have as an adult, although, of course, he has neither the information nor the exercise that will allow him to get the most out of those skills.

In fact, this speed of appropriation of the various levels of brain skills, developed and practiced over millennia, as we can see in Figure 1.3, it is mainly responsible for the underutilization, by man, of all the mental potential at his disposal, both at the emotional and operational levels and at the intellectual levels.

Scientists and philosophers went so far as to say that, under normal conditions of life and work, man does not use more than 20% of the intellectual and energetic potential of the brain placed at his disposal.

It is not difficult to imagine that if modern man were forced to live for a few years relying exclusively on his limbic skills before gradually and slowly assuming his cortical and neocortical skills, he would have time, need and opportunities to explore to the fullest each of the skills contained in these levels to reach adulthood with the experience and training necessary for the broadest and most optimized use of all their skills and abilities.

The main opportunity, in this sense, occurs in early childhood, from the moment the child is born, when he can only learn from the skills contained in the lower brain levels.

Exhaustive training of the potentials at this level is the key to the full use of all brain skills.

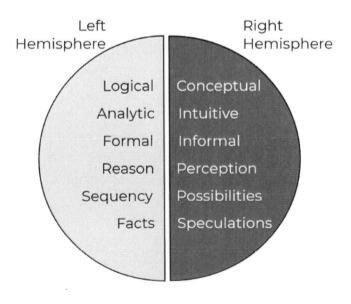

Figure 2.1 Cerebral Duality

2

The two hemisphere Brain

Since antiquity, innumerable researchers and scholars have looked into the analysis of the human brain skills, producing proposals on which concepts have been built that only over the last few decades have managed to become popular.

The first proposal to gain notoriety was the one related to "cerebral duality", implying the distribution of specific skills between the two, left and right, brain hemispheres.

According to this proposal, the left hemisphere would house concrete, logical, formal and analytical reasoning, based on reason, sequence and facts, with the right hemisphere having abstract, conceptual, informal and intuitive reasoning, based on perceptions, possibilities and speculations (Figure 2.1).

For many years, this theory about the distinctive ability of the left and right brain hemispheres to reason and provide critical / analytical and artistic / creative responses to human problems has received little new collaboration.

In contrast, the number of scholars using these concepts to support works, lectures and training and personal development programs grew year after year. Interestingly, most of these works focusing on the development of creativity (right hemisphere) more than any other brain skill, as if the left hemisphere deserved to be repressed in favor of the "magic" hidden in the right slice of the human brain. The logical and formal reasoning was treated as an undesirable inhibitor of creativity and the disciplinary and organizational inclinations as conservative obstacles to the processes of change, development and progress.

In the second half of the 1980s, Ned Herrmann, shed new light on the theories of left or right brain dominance, by proposing the metaphor of the four brain quadrants: upper left and right and lower left and right.

In Herrmann's proposal, four distinct groups of "brain preferences" or "thinking styles" can be identified:

✓ The rational (upper left), who analyzes, quantifies, is logical, critical, realistic, likes numbers, understands economic issues, knows how things work.

✓ The safeguard (bottom left), which adopts preventive actions, establishes procedures, does things, is reliable, organizes, is neat, punctual and plans.

✓ The sensitive (lower right), who is sensitive to others, likes to teach, touches people, is supportive, expressive, emotional, speaks a lot and feels.

✓ The experimental (top right), who conjectures, imagines, speculates, takes risks, is impetuous, breaks rules, likes surprises, is curious and plays.

The Ned Herrmann Group has developed a series of tests for self-assessment of the "brain dominance" of different individuals and has compiled, over the past twenty years, an impressive statistical sampling demonstrating how people's lives and professional trajectories are guided by their dominant skills.

Richard Bandler and John Grinder, analyzing the systems of representation and communications of the human being, laid the foundations of Neurolinguistic Programming (NLP) which attacked the universe of speculations regarding the possibilities of reprogramming, mastery and development of interests, skills and intellectual skills, applied to the field of communications and transaction analysis.

Bandler and Grinder did not elaborate in depth the correlation of NLP with the transactional analysis proposed by Eric Berne with the brain quadrality proposed by Ned Herrmann or with the seven types of intelligence described by Howard Gardner, ending up inaugurating a new autonomous discipline.

Studying deeply the cerebral duality proposed in the metaphor of the right and left hemispheres, the quadrality described in Herrmann's model and the triple representation system elaborated by NLP, we came to the conclusion that none of these models could explain in a complete and comprehensive way the development phenomena of human brain skills and skill differences between individuals (Figure 2.3).

More than that, we understand that they were not able to establish a logic for the mechanisms of evolution of the human mind over the generations, or throughout the life of each individual in particular.

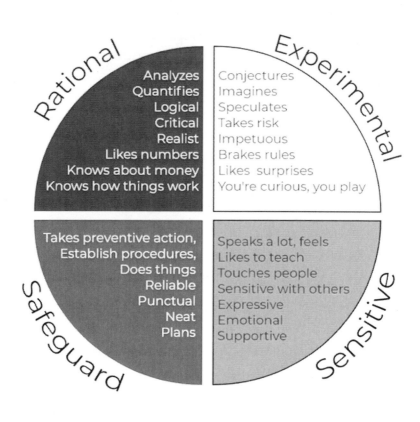

Figure 2.2 The four quadrant brain (Ned Herrmann)

These proposals, however, left open spaces for a more detailed analysis of the clusters of brain aptitudes as responses to the survival needs of species and to the vocation and dominance of some species over others.

In this space, we developed the proposal for cerebral multipolarity and its connotations, described along the next chapters.

3

The Concept of Cerebral Multipolarity

The development of the incipient pre-reptilian brain, with abilities limited to the actions of eating and procreating, took place in two directions (Figure 3.1).

For the left side, skills related to preservation grew to individual protection: reaction and escape.

To the right, gregarious skills aimed at guaranteeing survival through association with others approximation and grouping have grown.

With this conformation and skills, we find most of the known animals, mammals or not.

Action, reaction and escape, coexistence and grouping are common behaviors for mammals, reptiles, birds and other species. And none of these skills requires intellectual elaborations like those proposed in the cerebral cortex.

These skills are sufficient to provide for the livelihood of any living being in an lower environment competitive or threatening.

Observe the alligators. Its movements are abrupt and without any refinement. They can be found in flocks, but do not maintain any associative activity.

They can fight for a piece of food or leave it for the strongest. They live outdoors, without any concern for shelter.

They act, react, flee, live and group. But they dont live as families. The chicks, when hatch, are already entirely on their own. And they run the risk of being devoured by their own parents.

Chicken already seem a little more social. Than alligators they still move by leaps and make no associative effort. But they support their litter, helping them to scratch food until the they become self-sufficient.

Many birds take the food to the chicks' mouths.

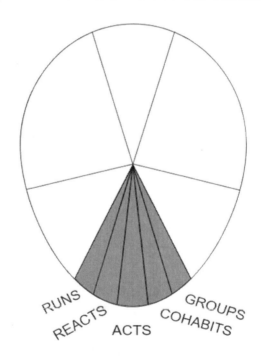

Figure 3.1. Instinctive Pole

Chicken use nests and shelters that are prepared for them. Most birds make their own nests and even shelters.

Birds and mammals have developed a "second

generation" brain system, including, on the left side, the search for shelter (burrow or lair) and the "mobilization of resources" (nest or bed) and, on the right side, association skills, including extra-sexual physical contacts and communication through sounds (paralanguage).

All mammals have a brain system more evolved for social skills. They breed the puppies in their womb, care for them after birth and breastfeed them throughout childhood.

Many wild animals hunt in packs and teach their children to hunt.

They all exhibit a wide variety of behaviors involving extra-sexual physical contacts and are able to learn to perform surprising tasks.

Monkeys carry their children on their lap. And they are seen removing head lice from their partners. It is true that they eat lice, but this is a way to combine the useful with the pleasant.

If not, they would have no one to take the lice off their own backs.

Monkeys, as already seen, although they do not produce tools, can improvise some and learn to use others.

The level of brain conformation and aptitudes of the monkeys is no longer common to most animals and has developed markedly in the first groups of primates that, fleeing dense forests, more than two million years ago, begun to live grouped in caves and makeshift shelters in the steppes and mountains.

It is exciting to imagine the extraordinary challenges faced by these ancestors closest to man for survival outside the forests.

Their upper limbs, more advantageous than their

legs, lost much of their usefulness in an environment where trees and vines were scarce and did little to help them in their walks or escapes, since, for many generations, they no longer functioned as "front legs".

Felines moved at least twice their speed and could hunt them much more easily than gazelles and other quadrupeds.

Fruit, tuber and insect eaters, with small teeth and weak jaws, they had to, long before discovering agriculture, become nomads in search for food and expand their limited carnivorous skills to compete with much more specialized predators.

They needed brain skills that could make up for these differences. They needed a cerebral cortex (Figures 3.2 and 3.3).

The first cells of the cerebral cortex brought, on the left side, self-discipline, self-control of deliberate actions and movements, and then, the ability to think about their actions (to plan).

On the right side, aptitudes came for reciprocal social support, for the transmission of knowledge, experiences and, therefore, for complete emotional and social involvement between groups, which could only be carried out in depth with the emergence of spoken language and writing.

The fossils of homo erectus, dating back more than 1.5 million years, exhibit a skull box much smaller than that of the modern man with the forehead still projected backwards, revealing less brain mass in the frontal region of the skull.

The Java Man with fossils dating back more than 500,000 years still had a low forehead and a small brain. The Peking Man, related to the Java Man, less than 300 thousand years old, already had greater cranial capacity.

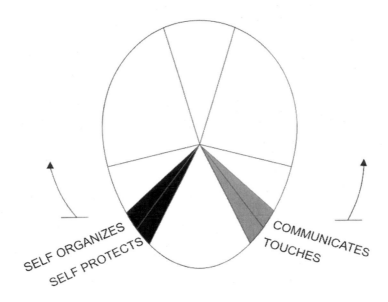

Figure 3.2. Pre cortical Operational Poles

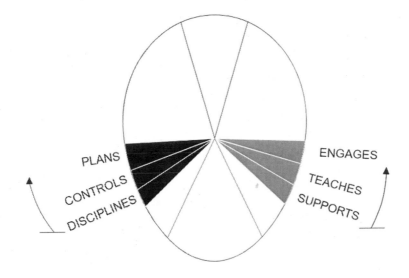

Figure 3.3 Cerebral Cortex

Nearly between the Neanderthal Man and the Cro-Magnon Man, separated by 30 thousand years of evolution, the cranial capacity reaches the dimensions of that found in modern man.

Homo-sapiens evolved into the social animal par excellence, starting with "breastfeeding" their children until adulthood.

The neocortex made room for intellectual exercises.

Analysis, quantification and criticism, evaluation and understanding on the left and imagination, speculation and the ability to infer and almost guess on the right side

These capacities (Figure 3.4) constitute the intellectual aptitudes of man, responsible for the superior capacities to reason, understand, create and combine knowledge and ideas of all kinds, generating, more and more, new knowledge and new information, in conditions to print, as they are printing, an exponential growth rate for knowledge.

It is evident that man does not yet know or understand a multitude of things. Starting with the "small space between our ears", as Bill O'Brien said, * and the infinite space we inhabits – the universe.

It is possible that help is on the way.

There is no indication that the human brain and its abilities have stopped growing and developing.

On the contrary, the most logical thing is to realize and admit that the brains of all species continue to evolve and that, the more evolved they are, faster is their rate of evolution (Figure 3.5).

Only this perception can explain why the skills of reptiles have evolved so little, in millennia, when compared to the skills of mammals and, particularly, of man.

It seems very clear that the use of our brain skills is progressively accelerating. The pace of scientific inventions and discoveries, going on an exponential scale, is the best evidence of this.

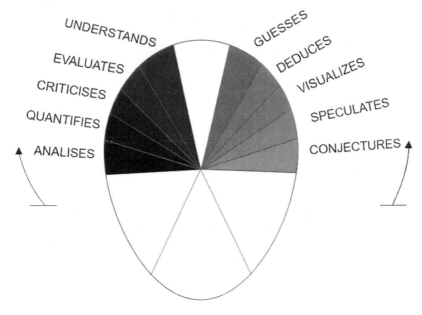

Figure 3.4. The Neocortex. Intellectual Poles

The man is learning to use his mind. Increasingly faster. And creating new needs for real expansion of its capacity.

It is important to note, however, that a real and more rapid expansion of our intellectual capacity involves rescuing all of our limbic abilities. Man cannot only exchange his most ancient and operational skills for new intellectual skills.

Scientific progress has greatly enhanced the

intellect, often at the expense of emotions new knowing at the expense of experience. Knowledge at the expense of wanting.

Many scientists already advocate the end of traditional offices and workshops with people working together and even traditional schools with people studying together, and their replacement by hermits in front of their computer screens, interacting only electronically.

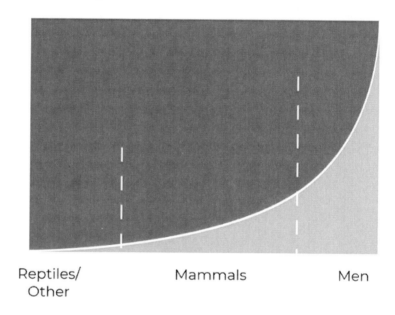

Reptiles/   Mammals   Men
Other

Figure 3.5 Evolution of the brain and brain skills

However, man cant do more and deserve more than that. By fully mastering all of his skills, he will be able to view broader horizons and more relevant values to consciously build purposes for greater personal fulfillment, both material and spiritual, and live happier.

The brain system of the most well-known animals

and man is frankly "operational".

Take the dog, for example. Like human ancestors, his preferred system of representing the environment is smell. He has this sense much more developed than man, being able to detect the presence of a milligram of a female dog urine dissolved in more than 100 liters of water.

The saying "More lost than a dog falliny from a moving truck" has its origin in the fact that a dog that has walked dozens of kilometers on an unknown path, even in the dark or with blindfolds, will be able to return to the point starting, sniffing his own steps.

See the horse. Vision is his strongest sense. His eyeball is larger than that of any other animal (larger than that of the whale). With one eye on each side of the head, he has a 360 degree view, being able even to see the rider mounted on him.

Moving both eyes forward, he assumes the typical bifocal vision of man and, although he has a monochromatic vision, he sees much further and with greater clarity.

He also has a luminous film on his eyelids that guarantees him a night vision far superior to that of man. His ability to detect small movements that would go unnoticed by the man is remarkable (that is why he is frightened by sudden movements).

Standing objects do not make any sense to him, since his vision is totally centered on movements that could represent a threat (a snake moving slowly in the grass) or opportunity (a branch of vegetation, which will serve as food, moved by a gentle wind).

Prehistoric man came to be as good or better than many animals in using limbic skills. He was certainly much better than we are today.

The passages mentioned in the stories, and reproduced in the cinema, about the use of indigenous guides to see and smell signs that modern man cannot identify are not fantasies. They are real facts.

When assuming new capacities and new interests, the human being ends up leaving behind and losing capacities that were very prominent and important for their survival and development.

In fact, basic skills have always given, can and will give, fundamental support for the full use of the superior intellectual capacities that man has developed. Therefore, he cannot do without them. It is necessary and important to value all of our evolutionary heritage and fully explore the skills with which nature has provided us.

The full use of brain skills maximizes our performance in all daily activities, with a great emphasis on teaching and learning processes, including in the education of our children, communications, coexistence and teamwork, leadership at work and family and business management.

In the modern world, we have become accustomed to looking for solutions to our problems in the specific teachings of third parties and this is good as it allows us to expand our wealth of knowledge.

What we must do is use, in addition to all the information from third parties that we can gather, our own intelligence and our own aptitudes.

All evolution have been, is and will be governed by competition.
There is no real evolution in non-competitive or abundant environments.

4

The Post Cortex and the QuaD Aptitudes

You have certainly heard of the unconscious and subconscious many times. And knew it before or realize it now that they refer to information stored at the deepest levels of the human central nervous system, much of it inherited from our most recent or most remote ancestors. Have you heard of "supraconscious"?

Scientific treaties, when studying the superior intellectual functions of the prefrontal association area of the neocortex, inform that:

"For many years, it was thought that the prefrontal cortex would be the location of the higher intellectual functions of the human being, mainly because the biggest difference between the brain of monkeys and that of humans is the great prominence of human prefrontal areas.

At the moment, despite all efforts, it has not yet been possible to show that the prefrontal cortex is more important than the other brain areas in higher intellectual functions. Furthermore, it was found that the destruction of the language comprehension area, located in the Wernicke area (further back and below) causes greater damage to the intellect than the destruction of the prefrontal area"...

What does that mean?

In the proposal for the development of brain skills contained in the figurative model we have designed up to this point, the prefrontal region would be the domain area of a cortical portion not yet fully developed or used: the "post-cortex", housing supra-intellectual aptitudes, not yet clearly identified or understood (Figure 4.1).

We conclude that this is the region of domain of the purely "spiritual" aptitudes of the human brain: spontaneous cognition, clairvoyance, telepathic capacity and other supra-intellectual variables, seen today as supernatural.

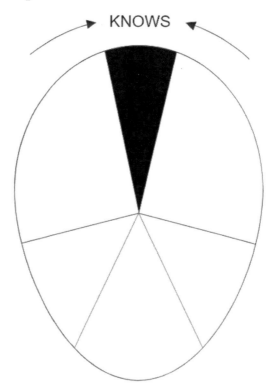

Figure 4.1. Supra Intellectual Pole. The post-cortex

"It becomes evident that the man's brain and the skills it contains are growing* over the centuries and millennia of evolution of humanity, in such a way that capabilities and 'powers' still little identified and used may emerge naturally in the far future

These almost divine skills, for which we are coining the expression QuaD (derived from "quasar" or quasi-stellar) already exist and already manifest themselves in the human brain spontaneously and, many believe, in a controlled way, explaining a series of phenomena seen as supernatural (and external to man) and even the origin of many beliefs and religions.

We cannot and do not intend to prove or demonstrate this.

Broad currents of parapsychology claim that man is already in possession of all the brain capacities focused on here, although he cannot deliberately dispose of them.

In these capacities, parapsychology includes knowledge phenomena classified as extranormal, paranormal and telepathic and the physical forces of the mind.

However, in the simple fact of treating these capacities as abnormal, including the documentation of many of their manifestations as pathological states, parapsycology recognizes, in fact, that such

---

* *The reference to the size and growth of the brain does not necessarily regard to its physical dimensions.*

abilities are only potential for the absolute majority of people.

From our part, we prefer to view these skills in the context of the capabilities still developing in the human brain (QuaD skills) and to propose attempts at understanding or direct and immediate access them.

We understand that they are poorly developed and used by most human beings.

And we believe that this is why science has succeeded in proving that *"the destruction of these areas causes less damage than the destruction of... older areas"*. It seems logical to us: The destruction of areas of the brain that harbor functions we use intensively (such as language understanding) do more damage to the known intellect than the destruction of areas that harbor functions which we rarely use (shelters of the unknown intellect).

We view this area of the cerebral neocortex as an "intellectual soft spot" that will close and complete in skills over time (millenia) in order to be used naturally and extensively by the man of the far future. Both lay people and scientists have come across strong evidence for its existence and functioning, but the lenses of science have not yet been decidedly focused on it.

We compared the future official discovery of the supraconscious with the discovery of the planet Neptune (eighth planet in the solar system on the scale of the Sun's remoteness).

Until 1846 only seven planets in the solar system were known, with Uranus being the most distant.

Unlike other known planets, it did not maintain a strictly elliptical orbit. Disturbances in Uranus' orbit led astronomers to imagine the gravitational pull of a neighboring planet, which they could not see.

Through mathematical calculations, frenchman Leverrier deduced the position of this hypothetical planet in space and passed the information to astronomer Galle, in Germany. Galle aimed his telescope at exactly the indicated point, and there it was: Neptune.

The same is true of the post-cortex and supra-intellectual skills. We cannot see them, but we have evidence of their existence due to the disturbances they cause in the known intellect: the known aptitudes, in the medullary, inferior or superior cerebral levels cannot explain a great variety of persistent phenomena occurring with human beings.

And the way out has been to attribute these phenomena to God, to saints, angels and spirits.

Without any conflict with these beliefs, we can say that a part of the powers attributed to God, to saints, angels and spirits are contained in the brain of man. In its noblest, newest and least known position. At the opposite pole to the crudest, oldest and most recognized nucleus.

This is the post-cortical pole, depository of man's supra-intellectual aptitudes, whose process of conscious access cannot yet be spelled out.

We are convinced that the mystical exercises of concentration and development of fantasies, proposed in most texts and books that dealt with this theme in some way, are not capable of producing clear or more than incidental results.

Some people, on some occasions, will access or have the impression that they have accessed unknown powers, but they will rarely be able to repeat the process at their leisure.

Most people, for the most part of incidents, will experience nothing more than frustrations or the feeling of inability or incompetence to master the powers of their minds.

In fact, the often frivolous approaches when not quackery (misleading) given to addressing this issue in dozens of books and conferences has contributed much more to make people feel unable to dominate their minds than going able to do so.

Best-sellers, authors and lecturers,
around the world, presented formulas
and exercises through which people could
manage the development of their talents.
It seemed so easy that it left, with most
readers, nothing more than
a feeling of inferiority
in front of these gurus.

5

The Poles (Cardinal Points) of Talent

The proposed evolutionary sequence ends in a brain that houses six different skill groups (Figure 5.1):

1. Corporal/Visceral (S)

Innate (instinctive) and cultivable physiological capacities to activate the motor organs and the senses (sight, hearing, touch, smell and taste) to perform movements and interactions essential to the preservation of life.

Typical in this area are mechanical and motor, sensory, physical / organic and athletic skills.

The characteristics of spontaneity and agility of reaction (reflexes) and the temperaments aloof (left side) or gregarious (right side), harsh or calm, harsh or peaceful, but always telluric (linked to the land and nature) belong to it. Good health and physical strength, more developed senses of touch, smell and taste also tend to be associated with this group of skills.

2. Preventive/Organizational (SW)

Innate and cultivated (learned) operational capabilities to direct actions to improve living and safety conditions through the mobilization of resources and their conservation (savings).

Typical in this area are administrative and bureaucratic, disciplinary and controlling skills, including the ability and interest in ordering things in sequence and planning.

The characteristics of punctuality and care, austerity, prudence, sobriety, restraint and conservative, methodical, suspicious, severe and spartan temperaments belong to this group.

Energy, tenacity, persistence, a more developed sense of vision, resistance to discomfort and tiredness are also often associated with this group of skills.

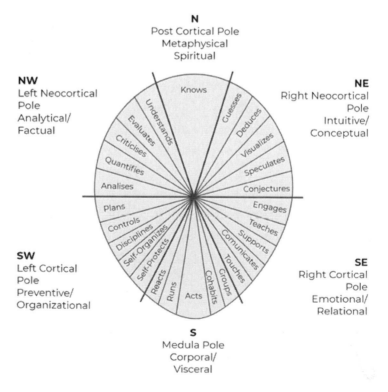

Figure 5.1 Full Brain Skills

3. Emotional/Relational (SE)

Innate and cultivated operational capacities to direct actions for the collective effort to improve living and safety conditions through community cooperation.

Typical in this area are the skills for communication and involvement with people, public speaking, teaching and charismatic leadership.

The characteristics of courtesy, emotionality, sensitivity, sentimentality and romantic, affectionate, outgoing, talkative, cooperative, empathic, conciliatory, humanitarian and lavish characteristics belong to this group.

Superior abilities to love and feel, support, educate and stimulate people, interpret behaviors, communicate through signs and achieve high performance in team activities and collective sports are also often associated with this group of skills.

4. Analytical/Factual (NW)

Innate and cultivated intellectual capacities to develop proposals for the optimization of living conditions, satisfaction, comfort and well-being, through understanding and mastery of the environment.

Typical in this area are the skills to understand the parts of a whole, correlate and interpret data, evaluate and diagnose concrete situations, develop logical reasoning and prognosis for the future.

The characteristics of rationality, perspicacity, strong pragmatism and introverted, cold, controlled, critical, calculating, materialistic and arrogant characteristics belong to it. Superior abilities to reason and solve complex mathematical, technical or economic problems, to understand concretely the physical and mechanical phenomena, more developed senses of vision and hearing are also associated with these aptitudes.

5. Intuitive/Conceptual (NE)

Innate and cultivated intellectual capacities to correlate ideas and sensations developed intuitively apart from facts or concrete data, to formulate hypotheses of motor responses optimized for the stimuli of the environment and to model it according to established conveniences or desires.

Typical in this area are aptitudes for abstraction, imagination, speculation, creation, invention and elaboration of spatial reasoning.

The characteristics of simultaneous reasoning belong to this group, a taste for adventure and risk, wit, cynicism, daring and the most cheerful and playful, impulsive, dreamy, fantastical, visionary, bold, detached from money and even people, but lovers of beauty and art in all its manifestations.

Superior abilities of holistic perception (view of the whole more than of the parts), creation of allegories and metaphors, elaboration of syntheses, resistance to frustration, senses of hearing and interpretation of more developed sounds are usually associated with this group of skills.

6. Metaphysical/Spiritual (N)

Latent and potentially cultivable supra-intellectual capacities to receive information in an extra-sensorial way, to know independently of analysis (a priori) and to understand the nature and the meaning of life and things for the maximization of man's spiritual potential.

Typical in this area would be the aptitudes for pure and transcendental philosophy, spontaneous cognition, premonition, understanding of universal (time and space) and supernatural (God and soul) phenomena.

The characteristics of spirituality, clairvoyance, mediumship and absolutely calm and unwavering temperaments, unconcerned with daily life, alien to material problems and lovers of nature and all things, in its broadest sense, belonged to it.

Higher abilities to sublimate emotions, to see beyond appearances and horizons, who knows, to dominate events with the strength of the mind would also be associated with this group of skills, if it were possible to clearly identify and access them directly.

It is as if we had four brains* at our disposal and two more that we are unable to consciously trigger and control.

Our inability to interfere freely with the skills contained in the lower portion of the limbic system or medullary pole is evident: controlling the circulatory process and heartbeat, instinctive movements of reaction to shock and pain, for example, and muscle energy itself.

However, there are numerous reports of conscious interference in this area, particularly the demonstrations conducted by Indian fakirs and evidence that, consciously or unconsciously, we are able to introduce variations in the movements generated in these areas.

The most common examples are changes in heartbeat generated by purely emotional stimuli, when no physical effort is involved.

Dramatic examples are given by the increased resistance to pain and shock in situations of high tension.

The human being may faint when receiving, by surprise, a blow to certain parts of the head or lap, but will resist, in action, during a corporal fight, much more numerous and violent blows.

Likewise, he can be knocked down by a stray bullet of small caliber. But if he is advancing on an enemy who fires shots at him, unless hit at a vital point, he will likely reach his attacker before he falls.

In a resting situation, the pain equivalent to the tearing of an arm by the bite of a lion will cause a man to faint immediately. But, in a situation of corporal struggle with the beast, he will only faint if hit by one effective lethal blow.

If we were able to control the powers of the spinal pole, (S) we could either stop our heartbeat or rescue the fury and strength of our ancestors.

On the other hand, science has also found that the information received by humans is not stored exclusively in the different regions of the cortex or neo-cortex.

Most of the ancient information received by man (via heredity) is stored at the levels of the unconscious and the subconscious and can only be "unarchived" in very specific contexts, such as dreams, deep hypnosis, exacerbated commotion, etc.

The other brain that we are unable to activate consciously and freely is the post-cortical or supraconscious pole (N), the seat of our latent supra-intellective skills.

Despite all the statements and cases reported in the context of parapsychology or spiritualism, we were not faced with any evidence of access and controlled use of these skills.

We believe, however, that the exhaustive exercise of all known skills can lead to the threshold of these superior skills, without frustration or disillusionment.

Each pole of talent also functions as a
window through which man sees
the world around him.
Each of us has a favorite window
but none of us looks at the world exclusively
through that window.

6

How Man sees the World

Hardly any human being will observe and interpret the phenomena around him using exclusively the characteristic approaches of each of the poles of dominance.

The most common is that our reading system tends to be a compound, not deliberate but consequent of our diversity of amplitude of talents, of the perceptions brought through the different windows that condition the perspective of the systems of communication and interpretation, characteristic of the different poles of dominance.

This is good, on the one hand, because it provides human beings with a more diversified perception of the various environmental situations but limiting, on the other hand, because it inhibits a complete and integrated perception of these same situations.

If it should be possible to isolate, one by one, the windows through which we perceive the environment, we would obtain a pure and complete reading of the situations through each pole and, from the sum of the readings thus obtained, arrive, effectively, at a complete and clear reading of reality in its most different aspects.

Through the spinal pole, using only corporal/visceral skills, we would see, in all things, only its shape and movement, since, in addition to being color blind, we would have no idea of measures or quantities.

Such seemingly limiting faculties would multiply our ability to detect movements, abstract chromatic concerns, be it qualitative and quantitative and, thus, focus at the same time on a broader and deeper spectrum (greater lateral and distance view).

On the other hand, our visual limitation would be largely compensated by a much more acute hearing, free from interference caused by language perception: words would have no meaning for us, so that our auditory system would be totally dedicated to the interpretation of sounds, just as our vision would be more sensitive to movements.

This reality explains why studies conducted in the field of neurolinguistics have found that only 7% of the interpretation we make of information received face to face depend on the perception of language, against 38% of the interpretation of the paralanguage and 55% of the interpretation of body language.

Sight and hearing are much older than the language made up of words, phrases, sentences and prayers. Therefore, much more ingrained in the human spirit. Allong millennia, we communicated through signals and sounds. Modern language is still very new to us. It is almost in an exprcimental stage.

Also, our sense of smell, touch and taste, at the medullary pole, are much more acute, in such a way that perceptions in our daily lives concealed by our sophisticated vision or dismissed as irrelevant by cortical aptitudes would assume greater importance in the process of interpreting the environment.

Acople of workers died of intoxication in South America, in November 1994, trying to solve a problem in a water tank in a building, because they saw no danger or threat in the place. If they were using exclusively the skills contained in the spinal cord, they would not have even approached that location.

The tactile information brought through this pole would, likewise, be much more numerous and expressive: we would never need to touch or get too close to a hot or cold object to feel its temperature.

In summary, the environmental reading processed through the spinal pole would reveal to us all the functional/physiological values of things, that is, it's immediate utility for life, in the state they are.

Curiosity at the spinal pole is practically limited to the location of things in space: "where"? and its generic "what"? qualification.

Through the left cortical pole, using exclusively organizational skills, we would focus on the environment, first of all, the potential utility or usefulness of things to generate long-term security and comfort: shelter or shield, weapon, utensil or tool; chair or work station.

Using vision as our preferred sense of interpretation of the environment, we would be attentive to the shape and dimension of objects, their position, ordering and dynamics; light and shadow.

It was through the skills of this pole that men began to represent the universe through sequential and organized images, creating the rudiments of written language.

That is why this pole functions as a reader and interpreter of body language and written language, as well as spatial and temporal relations between things.

It adds to the heuristic concerns of the spinal pole a greater emphasis on qualifying the location of things and situations (what and where) and introduces the temporal question: When? essential to the development of a continued, longer-term view of environmental phenomena issues.

The sense of smell, taste and touch are still very developed, but they are no longer the determinants of the perception of the environment.

The spinal cord does not correlate things with each other. The cortical pole, on the other hand, imposes the questions of what, how much and when in addition to where, establishing a more detailed view of organization and sequence, providing the perception of the correlation between the various observed phenomena.

The environmental reading through this pole would give us a complete and exclusive spectrum of the productive/ operational values.

Through the right cortical pole, using exclusively relational skills, all our attention would be focused on people and their feelings and on the relationships that any living being or inert object could have with people: proximity, similarity, relationship, dynamics, harmony, plasticity, sonority, expressiveness, beauty, flavor...

Paralanguage, the communication through sounds, had its origin in this pole, as well as the subsequent phonetic representation of the images that gave rise to the spoken language.

The development of language, allowing man to represent the universe through images, made his ability to transmit knowledge, teach and associate information explode, definitively sealing the vocation of dominance of the human species over the others.

At the same time, it inhibited, in some way, the ability of pure analysis of the environment.

For the first time, everything that is observed and identified is given a name and a descriptive label under which it can be known, regardless of further observations.

As man has conquered a superior aptitude for teaching, the large majority of people have been released from observing and interpreting, on their own account, the environment.

The gregarious concerns added to the heuristic the question of identifying the agents of the situations: who? But curiosity, then, could already be satisfied by the placement to other people, through language, of the questions: what, where, when, how much and who.

The man observes other men more than the environment itself and seeks to remove from his coexistence, through communication and feelings (observation of attitudes and behaviors), more information than can be revealed by conventional senses.

In few words we can say that the values focused through the right cortical pole are essentially human/social.

Through the left neocortical pole, on the other hand using exclusively factual skills, we would objectively focus on tangible and measurable values: weights and measures, distances, parts and composition, functioning, monetary or comparative value.

The identification of things and situations, in this pole, always leads to a deeper analysis of their nature, origin and destiny.

The left neocortical raises, in addition to the questions what, where, when and how much, the question "how"?

Anything that cannot be objectively observed or touched, measured, weighted, contacted, evaluated or scientifically calculated will deserve to be recorded in this pole.

Observing a stream, identified at the medullary pole as a liquid to quench thirst, and at the left cortical pole as an inexhaustible source of resources of different natures for different purposes – bathing, fishing, moving the water wheel, etc., the left neocortical questions the origin of the watercourse and the very nature of the water and everything it contains.

Understanding the nature of things, the NW pole positions it self to control and modify them, if necessary.

The values focused on this pole are, essentially, technical /scientific.

Through the right neocortical pole, using exclusively conceptual skills, we would always look beyond things, trying to see beyond what the vision reveals to us, to listen beyond what the hearing allows us and to feel beyond what the touch and emotions suggest us: origin, raison d'être, past and future. What it is, what it is not, what could be, to what context does it belongs.

The right neocortical looks at the whole and almost never at the details. Thus, he manages to have a more holistic (global) view of the universe and the existing interrelationships and dreams of seeing much more. The great dream of the right (conceptual) neocortical is, effectively, to guess and to know everything, intuitively.

Using hearing, the labyrinth of the inner ear and imagination as his preferred senses for interpreting the environment, he will "close his eyes" to see and understand things better.

More than any other, he will be interested in modifying things in order to make them more useful, easier, more understandable, more stimulating.

His most frequently asked question is "why"?, but, before understanding the nature of things, he will prefer to speculate, invent or guess it's reason for being.

The values focused on this pole are, basically, aesthetic/ subjective.

Through the post-cortical pole, using only metaphysical/ spiritual skills – if we could do that – we would accomplish the dream of the right neocortical, achieving, at the same time, a full view of the core of all things, capturing it's essential values.

Immediate utility, form, social connotations, composition, measures and values, hidden potential and possible developments would, in a fraction of a second, be perceived and recorded, regardless of any analysis. Without the need for any observation or question.

Metaphysical/spiritual skills, if widely developed, would lead man to omniscience, to the knowledge of all things. He would know everything and learn everything simply by looking at things or thinking about them.

This, of course, we are unable to do. But the perception that the post-cortical view is a summation of all the others provides a very important and provocative perspective for the perspective of its activation.

It is possible to conclude that we can exercise and develop a lot our ability to observe and understand the things, people and events around us simply by applying to the environmental analysis, in a conscious and programmed way, each of the skills that we can control.

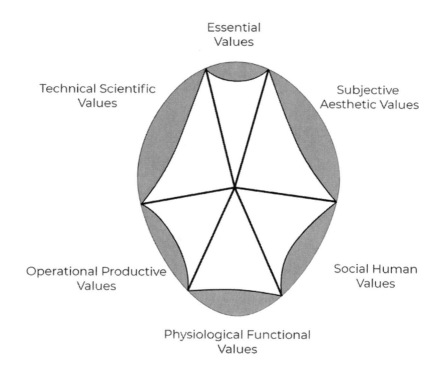

Figure 6.1 Windows and lenses for environmental reading

Try this every time you have a hard time understanding any phenomenon or other people's views on those phenomena. First, observe them spontaneously and naturally, without any concern to look and see more than you are used to seeing. Then, redo your observation using the characteristic approaches of each of the described "windows". Throughout and at the end of this process, you will have realized that you see much more and understand much more than you saw and understood before starting this exercise.

More than that, you will understand how and why other people see things differently.

And you will already know that you can dramatically improve your ability to understand all things and persons.

Perceptions, attitudes, and behaviors make the difference among men. Their place of birth is the brain. Their place of living is the world.

7

Theories of behavior in the light of Cerebral Multipolarity

Understanding the phenomena linked to the growth and variability of brain skills, in the form presented here, allows us to examine and see, in greater depth and richness of details, a wide universe of scientific knowledge and theories of human behavior.

In the light of brain skills, we can better understand the phenomena of neurolinguistic programming (NLP), the whole problem of human communication and the theories of motivation derived from the hierarchy of human needs proposed by Abraham Maslow, as well as the transactional analysis of Eric Berne, among many others.

We can clearly understand the differences in personality, ego or way of being and acting between people and the concepts of different types of intelligence and emotional intelligence.

We can also dare new reasoning to understand psychology and psychoanalysis, parapsychology and spiritual phenomena of all kinds, focused on sciences and religions.

We can concretely imagine the differences between body and soul and rationalize the concepts of soul immortality, reincarnation and memories of past lives.

We can do this without denying religious precepts and also without being totally dependent on them.

And, most importantly, we can take practical and immediate advantage of that understanding to help us to better understand everything and everyone, to help us to learn and to teach, to help us to communicate better, even with the most difficult people to treat. And to find greater pleasure in living with all of them.

This is an exciting journey that is worth undertaking.

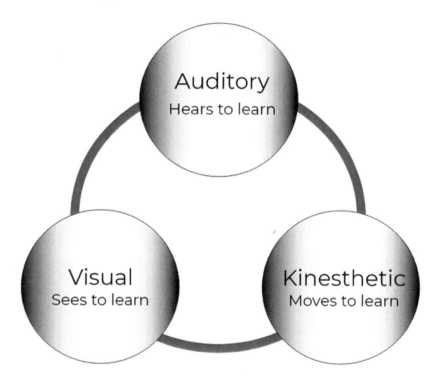

Figure 8.1

Three representation systems, according to NLP studies

8

Neurolinguistic Programming

The human being transmits and receives, interacts with the environment, through the five scientifically identified senses: sight, hearing, touch, smell and taste, and also through extrasensory receptors that could not be scientifically tracked or peremptorily denied.

In an objective way it appears that all the five known senses operate together in the communication process and that the importance of each one of them, as preferential means of contact with the universe, varies from individual to individual. It is as if we spoke five different languages and choose the one in which we are most fluent as our preferred language.

Hardly any of us would choose taste or smell as our preferred representation system for interpreting the environment, no matter how much respect we have for "man's best friend", who does this with mastery.

We would prefer our vision, our hearing and our tact (sensitivity) to receive and our voice and movements (including writing) to transmit.

NLP studies have indicated the existence of three types of people (Figure 8.1): visual, more connected in what they see (or read) and inclined to show or put in writing (or in figures) what they want to convey; auditory, more connected in what they hear and inclined to put in sounds and spoken words (to say) what they want to transmit; kinesthetic, more connected in what they feel and inclined to put in sensations and movements what they want to convey, whether speaking, writing or representing. NLP described, as well, a fourth system, the "Digital" described as a hybrid of the other three and characterized by the tendency to encode and decode messages in "data" using equations or expressions that facilitate more concrete evaluation and interpretation, logical and rational.

NLP did not say why people have a preference for these distinct systems of representation, but brain multipolarity makes it obvious.

The analytical/factual, within their tendency to value data and facts, numerical calculations and equations, interpret the environment and communicate with it through the digital system, which is not a hybrid of the other three, as proposed by NLP, but rather a autonomous system opposite to the kinesthetic to the point of refusing sensations and emotions in order to be able to focus on what can be demonstrated and proved.

The preventive/organizational ones, in order to give vent to their abilities to organize and control things, will need to be aware of the position of all things in space and, therefore, they will need to see and show, using the visual system, both to receive as to transmit.

The emotional/relational, confident in their sensitivity to people and the environment, will feel more comfortable transmitting and receiving through the kinesthetic system – they need to "feel" the adequacy of what they receive and make the adequacy of what they transmit.

The intuitive/conceptualists, wishing to speculate, imagine and guess, will not need to "see" things.

Their impulse to close the eyes or look away to better understand will make them aware of the meaning of the words and the sounds that support this meaning, both to receive and to transmit. This correlation brings into consideration the perception that the kinesthetic is not the opposite of the visual as proposed by NLP.

Although they are representatives of opposite cerebral hemispheres, left and right, they are "partners" at the same brain level, that is, more operational and emotional than intellectual ones, such as auditory and digital.

The real opposites are the auditory of the visuals and the kinesthetic of the digital ones, these, yes, representatives of opposite brain poles.

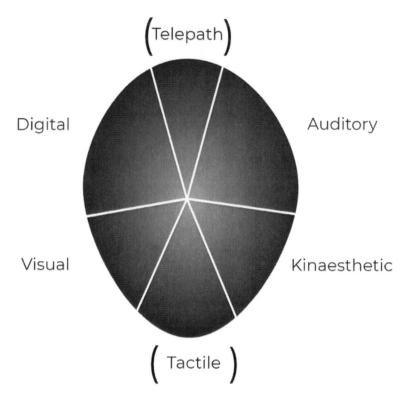

Figure 8.2

Neurolinguistics and representation systems (in the light of brain skills)

When referring to NLP, some texts suggest that the "preferred representation system" or "predominant sense of representation in the world" (Figure 8.2) can be diagnosed through evidence such as, for example, the profession: a good photographer is, almost always, the visual type; a musician, auditory. Or the physical type: a thin individual is usually visual; a fat, kinesthetic.

What would appear, at first glance, to be speculative or sample, takes on full meaning in the light of cerebral multipolarity. The emotional/relational is, due to its characteristics, the most likely to put on weight.

He is not kinesthetic because he is fat, but fat because kinesthetic. The preventive/organizational is, by its characteristics, the one that will better try to control his health and weight. He is not visual because he is thin, but thin because he is visual. In the same way, it is easy to see that the different dominances of brain aptitudes tend to guide and condition the professions chosen by people.

An athlete is not kinesthetic because he is an athlete, but vice versa; a musician is not auditory because he is a musician, but vice versa.

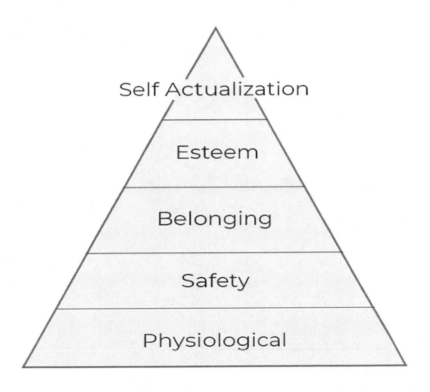

Figure 9.1 The Maslow Pyramid

The review of NLP concepts in the light of cerebral multipolarity lends greater depth to the understanding of individual differences, of the different ways of thinking and expressing, enhancing the performance of personal and group intercommunication and inter-cooperation.

9

Hierarchy of Human Needs

Psychologist Abraham Maslow proposed that all human beings feel, in certain measures, a set of needs that he classified as: physiological, safety, association, esteem and self-realization.

He also affirmed that most of the behaviors of each person tends to be dictated by the desire to satisfy his most intense need and that the intensity of the felt needs will vary in inverse reason to his satisfaction: the less satisfied the felt need, the greater the desire to satisfy it.

When analyzing the hierarchy of needs, proposed by Maslow, in the light of cerebral multipolarity and the sequential development of brain skills, from the bottom up and to the left and right sides, it is easy to understand the natural sequence of this hierarchy and the processes that trigger the different needs felt by the human being.

In the corporal/visceral pole, basic physiological needs predominate, whose attempt to resolve will occur, simply, through actions aimed at immediate survival.

In the pre-cortical poles, on the left side, we will find the safety needs, whose attempt to satisfy will occur through the effort to protect, in the long term, the conditions of subsistence, through the accumulation and organization of resources and, on the right side, the needs for association aimed, in the first instance, to guarantee long-term survival through community effort.

At the cortical poles the needs for position and power (which Maslow identified simply as status) arise and live in two variables: on the left, the need for dominance over others, which can be satisfied by the ability to discipline, plan and control the fate of third parties by virtue of possession of assets, resources or position; on the right side, the need for prominence characterized by esteem and admiration, whose attempt to satisfy will occur through the ability to support, teach, educate and get deeply involved with their fellow men (human virtues).

In the intellectual (neocortical) poles, individuals will be involved with themselves – in self-accomplishment projects that Maslow called "maximization of potential" – in two distinct sides: on the left, material, concrete and tangible self-realization, whose attempted satisfaction will occur through the maximization of the capacities to analyze, quantify, criticize and evaluate; on the right, the abstract and intangible "spiritual" self-realization, whose attempt to satisfy will occur through the maximization of the abilities to conjecture, speculate, imagine, create and infer (Figure 9.2).

This distinction characterizes two different groupings of needs for self-realization, not identified or described in Maslow's work.

The need for "maximization of potential" itself, the desire to get closer to divinity, to get as close to perfection as possible, to get as close to God as possible would appear in the last segments of the left and right neocortical pole and in the post- cortical (supra-intellectual).

This need could only be met by gaining the skills to understand, guess and know, in depth, regardless of prior information.

In the light of cerebral multipolarity, it is evident that the needs described by Maslow effectively maintain a logical "hierarchy" that reproduces, in modern man, the sequence of the emergence of different needs and the resources and aptitudes to meet them, throughout evolution.

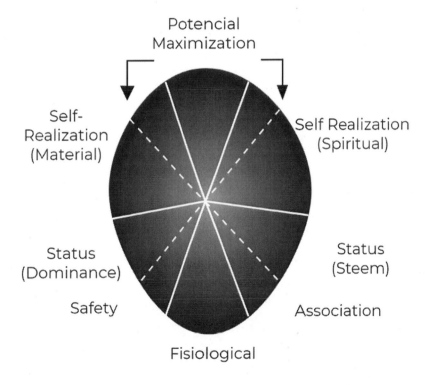

Figure 9.2.

The Hierarchy of needs in the light of brain skills

*The problem of low school performance
of the malnourished is not reduced
to a question of hunger or food
but to a matter of
specific needs that school meals,
poor or rich, cannot solve.
Malnutrition that inhibits higher
school performance is much more
psychological than physiological.*

10

Psychologically Malnourished

Crossing Maslow's theory with the analysis of brain aptitudes allows us to verify that, when feeling predominantly needs of existence and subsistence (basic physiological), security or association, people will be consistently moving their lower limbic and cortical aptitudes (operational and emotional) to produce immediate responses to those needs.

At the same time, it is clear that people whose basic physiological needs are already better met will be consistently moving their neocortical skills towards the realization of purposes of esteem and self-realization.

It is not difficult to verify that the substrates of the population represented by the upper-middle and upper classes, will have greater opportunities to connect with intellectual (neocortical) skills than the lower class populations. In these, activities, jobs and living conditions move, much more intensely, corporal / visceral, operational and emotional skills.

This situation produces sensitive results on the school performance of the middle and upper class populations compared to the low average school performance of the lower class populations.

And this has nothing to do with innate intellectual differences or with conditions of physical nutrition.

Someone has already said, to justify the difference, that "you cannot learn on an empty stomach" or that the undernourished have an intellectual performance lower than that of the well-nourished.

This phenomenon, analyzed in the light of cerebral multipolarity, may admit other responses outside the strictly food (or nutritional) field.

The problem of low school performance is not reduced to a question of hunger or food, but to a matter of specific needs that school meals, poor or rich, cannot solve.

Malnutrition that inhibits higher school performance is much more psychological than physiological.

With very few exceptions, the children of the poorest families experience, along with their fathers and mothers, uncles and grandparents, huge physiological and safety needs.

Their association needs also tend to be less met. They can have many friends and spend a lot of time with those friends exercising their relational skills and meeting their association needs.

However, many of them have limited contact with parents and family members – who work outside home, leave the house at dawn and arrive late – and precarious family integration in homes that are often troubled.

Having "their class" and their friends does not meet their association needs at the desired levels because most of them would really like to be better associated, attending groups and environments that they only know through television or "heard about".

These children and adolescents can be invited and even encouraged, at school, to use their superior intellectual skills to learn literature, humanities, physics or mathematics. But this will require them to move away, temporarily, from the more specialized skill hubs to solve their real problems.

Some pedagogues, attentive to the consequences of this phenomenon, regardless of the analysis of their physiological, psychological or social causes, propose and execute different approaches to the teaching of poor children, working with references and situations closer to their realities and environments.

Others have even proposed widely different curricula for subjects to be taught to these audiences, preparing them specifically for the occupations that seem most accessible to them.

This current has been repeatedly defeated by the perception that its proposals are reactionary and cruel, tending to maintain and confirm the inexorable status quo, preventing the poorest from having the opportunity to compete, on an equal basis, with students from the wealthy classes.

Of course, the situation cannot be solved in isolation by the school, but the prior and consistent analysis of the dominant skills among psychologically malnourished students can shed totally new light on the teaching proposals in this environment: selecting classes composed of students with similar skills and designating capable teachers to communicate effectively with these students to conduct programs specifically geared to making the most of the dominant skills in the group; adaptation of didactic resources for the teaching of the strangest subjects to their poles of dominant skills; develop specific proposals for school and professional training capable of compensating the difficulties of these groups and maximize the opportunities for success of each student in particular, in specific careers and professions demanded by the labor market.

Offering to psychologically malnourished equal opportunities does not mean lowering demands or directing them to simpler activities.

On the contrary, it becomes essential to enrich the educational and teaching processes and methodologies as to compensate their natural difficulties.

Our three ego states

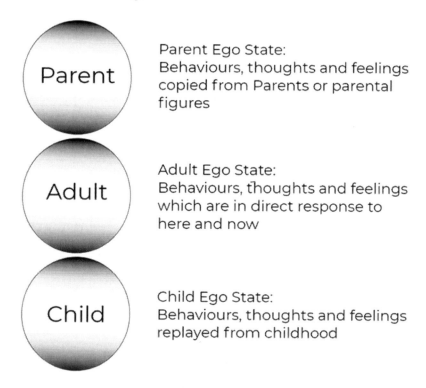

Parent Ego State:
Behaviours, thoughts and feelings copied from Parents or parental figures

Adult Ego State:
Behaviours, thoughts and feelings which are in direct response to here and now

Child Ego State:
Behaviours, thoughts and feelings replayed from childhood

Figure 11.1 Transactional Analysis – from Games People Play

11

Transactional Analysis

In 1951, Dr. Wilder Penfield, a Canadian neurosurgeon who developed a revolutionary technique for mapping brain tumors using an extremely fine needle, invited psychiatrist Eric Berne famous for his studies in the Freudian area (id, ego, superego), to witness some phenomena emerging in his work: when the probing needle reached deep regions of the brain, patients, in a conscious state, exhibited manifestations of return to childhood that disappeared when the needle was removed.

The rescue of subconscious memories was common in psychiatry, through hypnosis or chemical agents, but, for the first time, Berne was faced with the hypothesis that this information would be stored in specific physical planes of the mind.

The notes he developed from this experiment were decisive for the elaboration of the theses that would gain universal acceptance in the area of ego states and in transactional analysis.

According to the transactional analysis, the behaviors of individuals are governed by different states of ego that the psychiatrist called "parent", "adult" and "child" (PAC), with different subdivisions (Figure 11.1). These ego states would be the result of "recordings" made in the brain, started at birth and processed in the course of life.

In the parent ego state, the teachings and conduct of our parents or other parental figures with whom we live would be recorded: orders, recriminations, traditions, advice, morals, ethics, social rules, prejudices, teachings.

In the adult ego state, the behaviors resulting from intellectual elaborations would be recorded, with emphasis on:

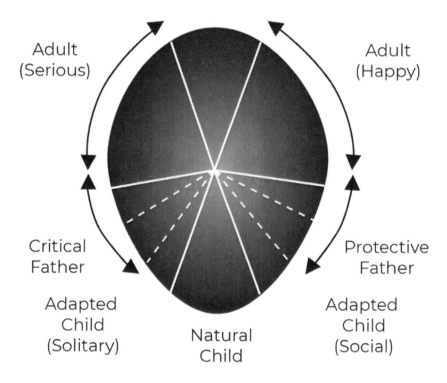

Figure 11.2

Transactional Analysis (in the light of brain skills)

current reality, rules of logic, objective data collection, information computation, analysis of reality data, organization and realistic programming, updating of parent and child data.

Emotions, feelings, timeless information, fanciful thoughts, sensibilities, impulses, creativity/ imagination, spontaneous behavior, magical ideas, pleasure and displeasure would be recorded in the child.

It is easy to see, in the light of the cerebral multipolarity that Berne cataloged, as a state of father ego, characteristic manifestations of the left cortical pole (preventive); as an adult, characteristic manifestations of the left neocortical pole (factual); as a child, characteristic manifestations of the right cortical and neocortical poles (the entire right hemisphere).

Through a deeper analysis of these manifestations, Eric Berne cataloged variables of the states of ego father (controlling or critical father and protective or nourishing father) and child (natural / free child, adapted child and small teacher).

In the light of cerebral multipolarity, it is possible to locate the critical father in the preventive pole and the protective father in the relational pole. The free child in the visceral pole and the adapted child in the organizational and relational poles.

It is also possible to see that the parent ego states are closer to the child ego states than the adult ones (the psychiatrist model would derive for APC – adult, parent and child) and, finally, the perception that the parent state adult ego would also include an intuitive / conceptual variable – a less circumspect and happier adult that Berne partially saw in the child's adult ego state.

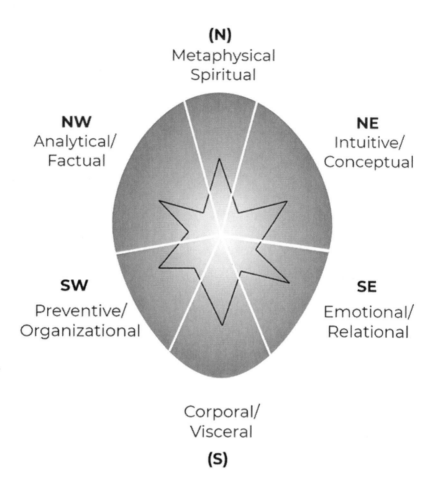

Figure 12.1 Multipolar Intelligence (the star graph)

12

Dimensions of Brain Skills

All the aptitudes described up to this point are contained in the brain of the modern man and "occupied" in this same sequence since his birth, assuming different amplitudes and intensities, from person to person.

The measure of breadth of brain skills refers to the variety of skills developed and exercised by each of us.

It is easy to see that all humans have the limbic abilities to act, react, flee, approach their peers and group with them. But it is easy to note, as well, that some prefer to flee or react while others approach and group.

Likewise, some people use mainly cortical skills of the left hemisphere: prevention, organization, discipline. Others experience the cortical aptitudes of the right hemisphere with greater pleasure: the physical and psychological relationship with other people, the pleasure of romantic life.

Neocortical skills are also used at different levels by different people.

Some are more concrete, logical, factual, numerical and detailed. They like to analyze, quantify, evaluate and understand.

Others are more abstract, intuitive, spatial and holistic. They like to imagine, innovate, speculate, infer, guess.

Thus, it is possible to identify different profiles of dominant skills in particular samples of humanity and different profiles of dominant behaviors displayed situationally by different individuals.

These differences are determined, first, by the comparative breadth of these skills – to the extent that each person uses, or prefers to use, throughout their lives or at different times and situations, the skills at their disposal.

Second, they are determined by the intensity and quality of those aptitudes. No two human beings are physiologically or psychologically identical. Each of us is unique in our way of seeing the world, being, thinking and acting.

The multiplicity of ideas or egos is easy to understand when we examine the different possible variables of skills distribution across the proposed groupings:

S – Corporal/Visceral
SW – Preventive/Organizational
SE – Emotional/Relational
NW – Analytical/Factual
NE – Intuitive/Conceptual
N – Metaphysical/Spiritual

The dominances at the S or N poles are only hypothetical, since they would represent, in the first case, a virtually instinctive (savage) human being and, in the second, a demigod (pure spirituality).

Regarding the dominance of skills in the poles under conscious control: NW, NE, SW and SE, the combinations are as varied as possible.

A person can be much more organizational (SW) than anything else. Or more relational, or more conceptual. In practice, it is not common to find people with extremely outstanding skills in a single pole, to the detriment of the others.

The most common profiles are the bi-dominant – especially more prominent in the sum of two poles: NW with SW (dominance in the left cerebral hemisphere) or NE with SE (dominance in the right brain) or NW with NE (dominance in the upper hemisphere) or SW with SE (dominance in the lower hemisphere).

Second, there are the tri-dominant profiles (higher scored skills relatively close one to each other, with only one secondary).

Multi-dominant profiles (great balance between the four poles) are even more rare.

In any case, two or more individuals with the same type of dominance in one, two or even three poles are unlikely to exhibit the same level of dominance in each of them.

The combinations of different percentages of dominance in each pole, only on a decimal scale (10%, 20%, etc.), would already lead us to more than three thousand possible combinations.

In order to represent, in a general and schematic way, the different basic profiles combinations of brain aptitudes, we created the "star" graph, using it to illustrate the descriptions below.

In these examples, we fail to mention the profiles of opposing dominances (NW with SE or NE with SW), which are rarer because they are representative of human beings experiencing great internal conflicts of ideas or ego:

SW / NE – extremely cautious and impulsive?

NW / SE – extremely cold and emotional?

Instead we've collected using the instrument and procedures listed beginning chapter 15 (page 105 on) of the most common profiles of teens and adults across Americas, Europe and Asia, during the past two decades.

Can you identify your profile?

Single NW profile – Analytical / Factual

Individuals who prefer to use it, like it better, feel better, working with the characteristic abilities of the left neocortical pole.

They are more concrete, cold and logical. Concerned with the analysis, evaluation and quantification of physical phenomena and it's full understanding.

They exhibit superior ability to reason and solve complex mathematical or economic problems and give exact value for money. They don't care much about people or their feelings.

They do not rely on their own sensations or feelings to make decisions and act, preferring to evaluate and ponder situations to rely on real and proven information.

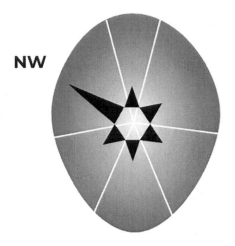

Analytical/ Factual

The NW are often introverted and serious, averse to intimacy with people who they do not know well and are almost immune to romantic or poetic daydreams.

They tend to belittle the sentimental and prefer to work alone.

They better accept and understand information based on data or that can be demonstrated in practice.

They want to demonstrate and prove when they transmit information.

Their predominant needs are oriented towards self-realization (maximizing their potential) in material, concrete and tangible terms.

Their transactional behavior reflects the state of adult ego, resulting from intellectual elaborations, with emphasis on evidence, rules of logic, objective data collection and combination of information for cold and calm analysis of reality data.

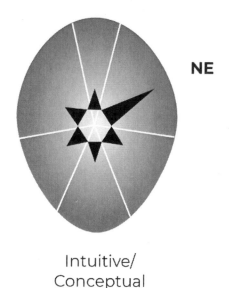

NE

Intuitive/
Conceptual

Single NE profile – Intuitive / Conceptual

Individuals who prefer to use it, like it better, feel better, working with the characteristic abilities of the right neocortical pole.

They are abstract, artistic and fanciful. Concerned more about generating than acquiring knowledge.

They exhibit superior abilities to correlate ideas and sensations developed intuitively to the margin of data and facts. They tend to be little attached to money and even to people from whom they rarely expect or demand reciprocity. They do not attach great importance to experience or real knowledge of past facts, preferring to rely on their own ideas and interpretations of the facts.

They have a taste for adventure and risk, making impetuous and often irresponsible decisions.

Driven by a rich and agitated imagination, they are often outgoing and playful, shrewd and cynical.

They are more resistant to frustrations resulting from their actions or the actions of others.

They better accept and understand information that leaves room for speculation and change. They prefer to have a global (holistic) than a detailed view of things.

They close their eyes to better understand the messages transmitted verbally and transmit through the meaning of words and sounds, as well as metaphors and allegories.

Their overriding needs are oriented towards spiritual and intellectual, abstract and intangible self-realization.

Their transactional behaviors reflect the child's ego, child, small master or adult state, committed to magical ideas, dreams, imagination and fantasy.

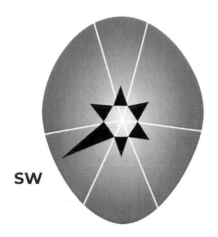

SW

Preventive/
Organizational

Single SW profile – Preventive / Organizational

Individuals who prefer to use it, like it better, feel better, working with the characteristic abilities of the left cortical pole. They are cautious, methodical and prudent. Concerned with the organization, ordering and control of things, information and activities.

They establish and adopt preventive actions and procedures and make things happen. They are reliable, organized, punctual and thorough in their work.

They mobilize and conserve resources (savers) and strive to fulfill their commitments with punctuality and rigor.

They have outstanding administrative, disciplinary and bureaucratic skills, including the ability and interest to work within established norms and plan for the near future.

They have little interest in creation, invention or speculation, preferring to work with established situations.

Little concerned with fantasies and averse to taking risks. They are often severe, suspicious and spartan.

They tend to exhibit great energy, tenacity, persistence and superior resistance to discomfort and tiredness.

Attentive to the position of all things in space, they want to see when they receive information or show when they transmit it.

Their overriding needs tend towards security (individual and family) and status (dominance over others). Parameterized by rules and learned norms, their transactional behaviors reflect the state of the father and adapted child ego: orders, recriminations, traditions, advice, morals, ethics, social rules, prejudices and counselling.

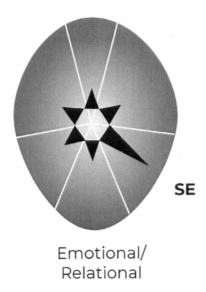

SE

Emotional/
Relational

Single SE profile – Emotional / Relational

Individuals who preferentially use it, like it better, feel better, working with the characteristic abilities of the right cortical pole.

They are romantic, emotional, affectionate. They are concerned with social organization and with the well-being and feelings of people and indifferent or antipathetic to the exact sciences.

They exhibit superior abilities to love and feel, to support their fellowmen, to teach, to stimulate people and to be involved with them.

They are outgoing, talkative, cooperative, courteous, empathic, conciliatory, humanitarian and lavish. They like to make friends, socialize and chat with them, work and have fun in groups.

They also like to take care of people and animals.

They are the greatest connoisseurs of music,

poetry and romantic stories, preferring interpretation more than creation.

They tend to be excellent interpreters of feelings and behaviors, although they can be deceived by their great confidence in people.

They get hurt more easily when they don't get the level of reciprocity they expect from others, developing feelings of insecurity and fear towards very cold and materialistic people.

They feel more comfortable and learn better the information transmitted with emotion (touching) and transmit better through emotions and feelings.

Their overriding needs tend towards association and esteem (of third parties).

Parameterized by their feelings towards people and things, they exhibit transactional behaviors that reflect the ego of the protective (nutritious) parent or social child.

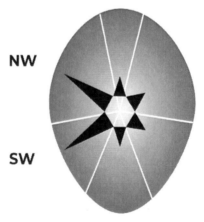

Tecnical/
Organizational

Bi dominant NW SW profile Technical/ Organizational

The technical/organizational profile identifies the individuals with the most pronounced aptitude dominance in the left cerebral hemisphere, hanging more or less towards the cortical (S...) or neocortical (N...) poles.

Its description combines characteristics of these two profiles, in different dosages that always emphasize logical, formal and analytical reasonings, attitudes and behaviors, based on reason, sequence and facts, with less participation of reasonings, attitudes and conceptual, informal behaviors and intuitive, based on perceptions, possibilities and speculations.

The technical/organizational profile corresponds, exactly, to the concept of the left cerebral hemisphere in the proposal of cerebral duality, being able to describe a more intellectual individual (NW skills) or more operational (SW).

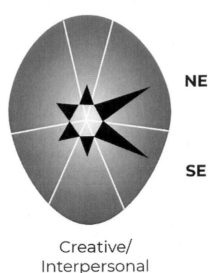

NE

SE

Creative/
Interpersonal

Bi dominant NE SE profile – Creative/Interpersonal

Creative / interpersonal is the characteristic profile of dominance in the right cerebral hemisphere, also with different combinations of cortical (S...) or neocortical (N...) aptitudes.

It is "the other side of the medal" in relation to the NW / SW profile, dominated by reasoning, attitudes and conceptual, informal and intuitive behaviors, based on perceptions, possibilities and speculations.

The creative / interpersonal combines, in smaller doses, skills of the NE and SE dominance poles, leaning towards one or the other: more thinkers (N...) than doers (S...) or vice versa.

The skills of these poles can also be quite balanced, identifying individuals with greater versatility of skills in these two poles.

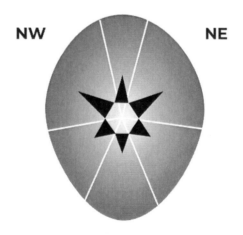

Intelectual

Bi dominant NW NE profile – Intellectual

By representing the intellectual profile, this

combination of talents identifies individuals with greater skills in the neocortical poles, capable of developing, with safety and comfort, both logical and speculative reasoning.

Their lower skill load at the lower brain poles indicates that they are more thinkers than doers.

They will, however, have a predilection for executive works that require neocortical talents such as artistic activities of different species: literature, music (including creation), drawing, painting, sculpture and all kinds of physical and manual work that are delicate or require distinguished abilities.

In fact, the intellectual dexterity of this profile transfers physical dexterity to refined movements, more than to any other bodily action. In general, the intellectual is not physically strong, nor skilled in physical / energetic activities. He has less resistance to physical tiredness and, in reality, "does not like to push".

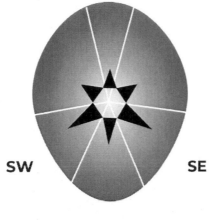

SW   SE

Operational

Bi dominant SW SE profile – Operational

The operational profile of aptitudes concentration at the cortical poles and the limbic system (S) is the opposite of the intellectual, as it is much more linked to action than to pure thinking. This does not mean that he does not think. On the contrary, he thinks a lot and operationally, that is, he thinks about the things that can and needs to be done and does them. His intelligence is therefore more practical and often more fulfilling.

Rarely any refined intellectual or bodily work that one perform will have the same "finish" as that produced by an intellectual. Its production volume will, however, be higher than that of the intellectual, especially in activities that require more striking physical effort.

The operational profile corresponds exactly to the emotional intelligence model focused on in Chapter 14.

13

The six kinds of Intelligences

As we have seen, the amplitude dimension of brain aptitudes refer to the different profiles of aptitude distribution in each individual configuring distinct levels of skill dominance from person to person.

Thus, by assessing the breadth of our brain skills, we can identify our dominant pole and establish the grading differences between each of our skill poles.

This will allow us to see the similarities and differences in skills and interests between various individuals.

However, when comparing two individuals with identical percentages of skills dominance in any pole, we can still find qualitative differences in the intensity of these skills.

Two people can be equally organizational and it becomes evident that the quality of the projects prepared by one of them is better than the quality of the projects of the other.

In the same way, it is possible that the quality of organizational work of the second individual comes to be superior to the quality of organization of the first.

These qualitative differences can be determined both by the information and experience accumulated by each of them and by their global level of intelligence

(Intellectual Quotient or IQ).

Until very recently, intelligence was seen and treated as a generic level of intellectual attributes of the human being.

Numerous tests of perception, knowledge, memorization and interpretation of information (psychotechnical or psychometric tests) were developed to measure the Intellectual Quotient (IQ) of children and adults, culminating in a global and unique score capable of comparing each to other and all of them.

Creative and holistic perception, logical and analytical reasoning, organizational vision and communication senses were not observed as separate and distinct phenomena in these tests.

Smarter or less intelligent was the result offered, until two types of intelligence, quantitative and qualitative started to be mentioned.

Howard Gardner, professor of education at Harvard, devoted himself to the task of researching and cataloging, among people seen as geniuses or mediocre, different types of abilities and aptitudes, concluding with the existence of seven types of intelligences, which he defined as:

• Linguistic intelligence: ability to speak or write well, extremely developed in great speakers and writers.

• Logical or mathematical intelligence: ability to think, calculate and handle logical reasoning, present in scientists, physicists and mathematicians.

• Spatial and visual intelligence: ability to paint, draw, sculpt, photograph with precision and art, advanced in great artists and also in navigators capable of orienting themselves only by the stars (1).

- Corporal-kinesthetic intelligence: ability to use one's own hands or body, highly developed in successful athletes and great actors.
- Musical intelligence: ability to compose songs, sing and play instruments (2).
- Interpersonal intelligence or social intelligence: ability to relate to others.
- Intrapersonal or intuitive intelligence: ability to access one's own intimate feelings.

(1) *Includes the concept of visual intelligence when referring to visual orientation seen at Gardner's proposal as spatial orientation (which does not refer to looking and seeing continually points of orientation).*

(2) *Musical intelligence in this context is seen as a combination of parts of spatial IQ, with organizational IQ and verbal/social IQ.*

This proposal allowed educators to refine the processes of evaluating the intellectual potential of children and adults correcting the deficiencies that, until then, separated them on a single scale as being more intelligent or less intelligent.

However, for educational and other purposes, it itself deserves some repairs.

The study of Gardner's proposals in the light of cerebral multipolarity suggests that it is possible to view, explain and understand, objectively, not seven, but six types of intelligences (IQs) anchored in the six different skill poles.

Spiritual IQ: measure of intensity of the post-cortical pole (N) skills related to the potential ability (therefore in parentheses) to recognize and know, intuitively and a priori, independent of information transmitted by third parties through the scientifically cataloged communication systems (vision, hearing, touch, smell, taste).

These skills include part of the concept proposed by Howard Gardner for intrapersonal or intuitive intelligence.

Spatial IQ: measure of intensity of the typical skills of the intuitive/conceptual pole (NE). Capacity for global (holistic) perception of situations, abstract reasoning and spatial orientation; imagination, creation and inventiveness.

These skills encompass some fundamentals of musical Intelligence and are not to be confused with the visual Intelligence proposal developed by Gardner.

Mathematical IQ: measure of intensity of the typical aptitudes of the analytical/factual pole (NW). Ability to reason logically, concretely and numerically, from the analysis of data, facts and correlation between them, for the elaboration of diagnoses and prognoses.

Organizational IQ: measure of intensity of the typical preventive/organizational (SW) skills. Ability to mobilize, organize and control resources and things, proposition and obedience to norms and rules of action and behavior, timing and care. Visual acuity for details and sequencing of actions.

Verbal/social IQ: measure of intensity of the typical skills of the emotional/relational pole (SE). Ability to associate and communicate with third parties, develop relationships and group activities, negotiation and leadership, which includes Gardner's concept of interpersonal intelligence.

Dynamic/body IQ: measure of intensity of the typical skills of the corporal/visceral pole, including the ability to control the body and movements (bodily/kinesthetic intelligence).

The skills for composing songs and playing instruments, put by Gardner in the same group, are skills that, in the light of multipolar intelligence, have very little kinship.

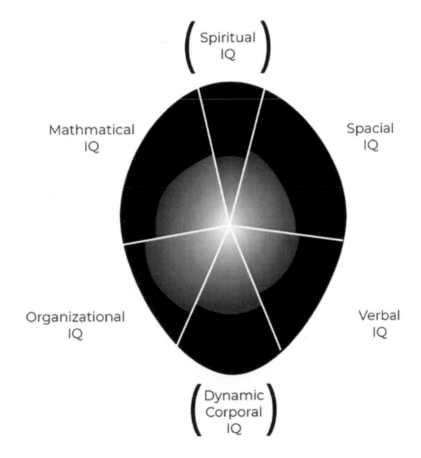

Figure 13.1 Kinds of intelligence – In the lights of cerebral multipolarity

"What factors come into play
when people
with high IQ flop and those of modest IQ
do surprisingly well?
I would say the difference is in the skills
here called Emotional Intelligence,
that include self-control, zeal and persistence".

Daniel Goleman in Emotional Intelligence

14

Emotional Intelligence

The perception of the existence of these various types of intelligences provides the logical support for understanding the concept of emotional intelligence developed and explored in the work of psychologist Daniel Goleman (October 1995) and, more than that, to make it possible to access, use and develop these skills through appropriate exercises.

The mathematical intelligence, or aptitudes typical of the analytical/factual pole (NW), allows contemporary man to analyze, quantify, criticize, evaluate and concretely understand the physical, chemical and biological phenomena with which he has always lived during all stages of its evolution.

Spatial intelligence, or typical skills of the intuitive/ conceptual pole (NE), opens up the possibilities for men to conjecture, speculate, imagine, infer and even guess the true nature of these phenomena.

However, to provide actions on these phenomena, we need to appeal to the typical skills of the preventive/ organizational (SW) and emotional/relational (SE) poles (operational and relational intelligence) that our ancestors, throughout millennia, have always used to manage or try to handle the same phenomena.

Our superior intellectual aptitudes, in other words, allow a better diagnosis of different situations, optimizing our perspective of more effective handling of all internal and external phenomena. But they, by themselves, will not lead us to act on these phenomena. (*The cerebral cortex mainly thinks... the limbic system mainly moves actions and reactions*).

Emotion, as Goleman observed, is much faster than reasoning and can, if not properly parameterized, "lead to both love and war".

Self-control, zeal and persistence are typical skills of the left cortical pole (SW) that human beings have developed as a basic condition for survival in a progressively competitive and threatening environment.

Humanoid primitives were smaller and weaker than contemporary man, as all archaeological finds prove.

Their legs were shorter and their arms were longer, suggesting a speed of travel not only lower than that of today's man, but particularly much slower than that of felines and canids, their natural competitors in hunting.

The first primates, driven by competitive instinct and oriented for their basic abilities of action and reaction, challenged and faced, with open chest and with enormous disadvantage of claws and teeth, these natural enemies.

They paid dearly and, slowly, generation after generation, a small light began to flash inside their minds: *"protect yourself..."*

The lairs, caves and natural shelters marked prehistory with the "cavemen". The first instruments of attack and defense identified the ages of stone, copper, bronze and iron.

Driven by the survival instinct, man began

to develop diversified operational skills. A type of intelligence focused on the mobilization and organization of resources in a rational process based on variable diagnoses of the different threats to be faced.

This process is very distinct from the purely instinctive processes of organization and mobilization of resources moved by ants and bees, for example, which do not contain any rational ingredient.

The zeal and persistence of bees and ants are capable of giving a "bath" in the zeal and persistence of the most legendary human fighter, but the zeal and persistence of insects are essentially "stupid".

Worker bees continually transport nectar to feed the larvae, but every beekeeper knows that he removes the larvae from the hive the insects zealously and persistently – mechanically and instinctively – will continue their task without realizing the futility of their work.

Many men often do the same thing when they do not put their intellect at the service of their emotions.

The pitfalls of emotional intelligence can be terrible.

The full use of brain skills, associating intellect and emotions, relies on the experience and speed of limbic skills and in the diagnostic faculties of cortical skills to produce the best composition of reason and emotion, maximizing the adequacy of the responses generated for the challenges of the environment.

This combination applies to enrich human performance in life and work, particularly in the processes of learning, communications and negotiation, teamwork, creative process, entrepreneurial process and management.

The challenge we have to face, then, is to activate, in the right measure, both the intellectual and the man of action that we have inside us.

What is the difference, in practice, between an intellectual and a man of action? We have all known, for many years, that the so-called "intellectuals" are more prone to reflection than to energetic and continuous action.

The taste for design is a typical characteristic of cerebral dominance in the upper hemisphere.

Individuals stronger in this position will tend to jump from project to project (see Entrepreneurial Process), not even trying to implement effectively most of them.

In the meantime, individuals dominant in the lower cerebral hemisphere will be constantly putting new ideas into action, even if superficially elaborated or poorly digested.

The very strong in this position can even persist in their actions throughout their life, without any impulse or desire for change, even when they are not being successful.

We cannot change our profile of brain dominance as we like because it was elaborated for millennia through heredity and for many years of our life through the education we had and the environment in which we live.

However, nothing prevents us from knowing and understanding our dominant and secondary skills, managing one and the other, accessing, using, learning to appreciate and even developing our ability to use different skills.

It all comes down to a matter of firm decision and persistent exercise. Starting on page 191, you will find complete batteries of exercises for the development of different skill groups: creativity, logic, organization and communication.

Performed seriously and in the appropriate frequency and sequence, these exercises will help you to significantly improve your performance in all areas.

- Your instincts, basic emotions and dynamism. Your corporal/visceral talents.
- Your precaution, discipline and organization. Your organizational talents.
- Your communication skills, relationships and empathy. Your social talents.
- Your logical thinking, concern with data and facts. Your critic talents.
- Your imagination, creativity and fantasy. Your creative talents.
- Your spirituality, intuition and refinement of concerns. Yor spiritual talents.

Some of the listed exercises will be pleasant and gratifying to you, while others may be hard to perform or tiring . It depends on your profile. Whatever the situation, always choose to begin with the easier ones and follow a scale of lowering difficulty towards the harder to develop and accomplish.

*The concept of "Emotional Intelligence"
refers to two types of intelligence – rational
and emotional, stating that*

*"The intellect cannot do its best
without emotional Intelligence".*

The concept of cerebral duality, known and well accepted for more than forty years, refers to the left and right brain hemispheres as the headquarters of logical and formal reasoning and of romantic and conceptual reasoning. Many authors have already referred to the dual reason and emotion to define the aptitudes of these two hemispheres (1)

The variation of this concept for the lower and upper brain hemispheres (more ancestral and more recent brain systems) began to be elaborated more than 20 years ago and has its scientific support in the knowledge about the evolution process of the central nervous system of animals and the man.

The concepts of cerebral quadrality and, in particular, Gardner's proposals for the seven types of intelligence interpreted in the light of cerebral multipolarity, explained in this book, add data of fundamental importance for broadening the understanding of all past, present and future brain skills of man.

The reduction of this concept to two types of intelligence – rational and emotional – is an imprecise simplification because the intellectual system is not only rational. He's rational and fanciful. IQ already involves at least two types of intelligence.

The concept of cerebral multipolarity, in turn, accurately exhibits the intellectual abilities of the human being in three poles of the upper brain system and the emotional (operational) aptitudes in three of the lower brain system.

This model also makes it clear that the intellect can not do its best without emotional intelligence and that this one can not do its best without intellectual support.

The vision of cerebral multipolarity guides the processes of bringing intelligence to emotion and, also, emotion to intelligence.

The concept of emotional intelligence, disseminated by Goleman, corresponds to the set of skills of the "operating system" of the brain.

The concept of emotional intelligence will be better understood – and better used – within the broader concept of cerebral multipolarity as above explained.

Which is your Profile?

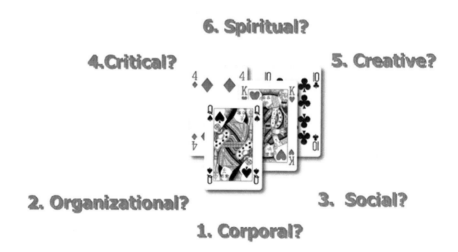

6. Spiritual?

4. Critical?   5. Creative?

2. Organizational?   3. Social?

1. Corporal?

Identify your Dominant Skills

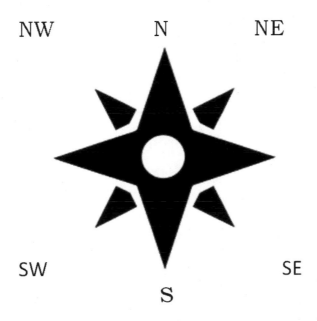

Fix your attention on this Compass Rose. It represents the six different brains inside your brain.

The upper pole (N = north) represents your spiritual, intuitive and conceptual brain, your pure imagination, your ability to elaborate abstract reasoning; your ability to know a priori things that were never transmitted or taught to you. It is the most noble and most recent part of the human brain, including even poorly known or explored capabilities.

The lower pole (S = south) represents your instinctual brain, your body and visceral skills, your energy, your dynamism.

The lower left pole (SW = southwest) represents your organizational brain, your skills for mobilizing and conserving resources, your discipline, your method.

The lower right pole (SE = southeast) represents your social brain, your communication and relationship skills.

The upper left pole (NW = northwest) represents your technical/scientific brain, your logical and concrete reasoning, your ability to deal with numbers and values; your analytical/factual skills.

The upper right pole (NE = northeast) represents your creative and artistic brain, your sensitivity, the refinement of your communication skills through different artistic manifestations such as drawing, painting, sculpture, music and many others. Imagine a deck of cards of six different suits. In addition to the normal Diamonds, Hearts, Clubs and Spades, you have two more suits in it. The Star and the Seed.

Each of these suits represents one of your six brains or talent hubs.

The Star, symbolizing the universe and mother nature, occupies the N position.

The Seed, representing your roots, instincts and energy, occupies the S position.

Swords, symbolizing science, occupies the NW position.

Clubs, symbolizing work, occupies the SW position.

Hearts, symbolizing love, occupies the SE

position.

Diamonds, representing the fortune and the arts, occupies the NE position.

Now, stop imagining and examine, on the next six pages, the cards in this deck numbered from 1 to 64 with two blocks on each page. Each card contains a descriptive sentence regarding a detail of each of the different human skills.

Choose, in each block (from the top half of the page and the bottom half) the card whose phrase best suits you.

Do not look for right or wrong answers and be careful not to choose cards that describe "what or how you would like to be". Don't even try to assemble a panel of everything you are, feel and do.

In each block, choose only the card that best applies to you. Mark the numbers chosen in the first column of a table like the one on the page 114.

Choose the card that best describes yourself

1 I like activities when I know everything about them

2 I like activities when the people involved work in harmony

3 I like activities that have clear rules

4 I like activities that are totally new and challenging

5 I like activities that require strength and energy

6 I like activities that involve art and creativity

Choose the card that best describes yourself

7 I don't like activities at which people involved argue and fight

8 I don't like activities that do not have practical use

9 I don't like activities that move slow

10 I don't like activities that cut my creativity

11 I don't like activities that involve routine work

12 I don't like activities that are messed up

Choose the card that best describes yourself

13 I work better when everything is well organized

14 I work better when I have concrete information

15 I work better when I have the opportunity to use my imagination

16 I work better when I can share my feelings with others

Choose the card that best describes yourself

17 When I want to convince someone I present data and facts that support my ideas

18 When I want to convince someone I always show things that they can read or see

19 When I want to convince someone I use images and illustrative examples

20 When I want to convince someone I try to reach people's hearts

21 When I want to convince someone I appeal to people's imagination and fantasy

22 When I want to convince someone I put a lot of enthusiasm and energy into my ideas

Choose the card that best describes yourself

23 I understand better and believe more when they show me and explain step by step

24 I understand better and believe more when there is art and creativity in the presentation

25 I understand better and believe more when ideas are presented with strength

26 I understand better and believe more when I empathize with the presenter

27 I understand better and believe more when my intuition confirms what I hear

28 I understand better and believe more when things make logical sense

Choose the card that best describes yourself

29 I'm more aware of what I hear

30 I'm more connected to what I see

31 I'm more aware of what I feel

32 I'm more connected of what I evaluate

Choose the card that best describes yourself

33 I find it easy to imagine things as a whole

34 I can easily understand how the parts combine as a whole

35 I can easily see the details that a lot of people don't see

36 I find it easy to act and react quickly to things that happen

37 I find it easy to be interested in people's feelings

38 I find it easy to create alternatives to ways of seeing things

Choose the card that best describes yourself

39 I like to be punctual and careful in everything I do

40 I like to evaluate and understand things well before giving an opinion

41 I like to relate to people and help them

42 I like to draw, paint, sing, and / or other types of artistic activities

43 I like to daydream and come up with new things

44 I like to play sports and have lot of action in everything I do

Choose the card that best describes yourself

45 I am guided by the saying: The more you know the less you cry

46 I am guided by the saying: A bird in the hand is worth two in the bush.

47 I am guided by the saying: No risks, no gain

48 I am guided by the saying: One swallow doesn't make summer

Choose the card that best describes yourself

49 I have a good artistic ability in at least one area

50 I'm very good at organizing and controlling activities

51 I get along with numbers and calculations

52 I am very efficient in the relationship with people

53 I am very energetic, fast and dynamic to get things done

54 I am very intuitive and able to see and understand things that I have never been taught

Choose the card that best describes yourself

55 I get bored with very "square" people

56 I get furious with lazy people

57 I get sad with ungrateful or rude people

58 I do not give much value to people who do not add their own ideas to known things

59 I get angry at disorganized or undisciplined people

60 I am inhibited by people who force too much intimacy with me

Choose the card that best describes yourself

61 I can spend hours philosophizing about the mysteries of life

62 I can move from calm to exasperation very quickly

63 I can hug a person I barely know

64 I can spend hours discussing technical issues

Watch the suites you chose

spades

1, 8, 14, 17,
28, 32, 34, 40,
45, 51, 60, 64

star

4, 10, 21,
27, 33, 43,
54, 58, 61

diamonds

6, 11, 15, 19,
24, 29, 38, 42,
47, 49, 55

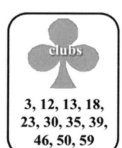

clubs

3, 12, 13, 18,
23, 30, 35, 39,
46, 50, 59

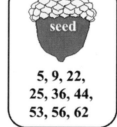

seed

5, 9, 22,
25, 36, 44,
53, 56, 62

hearts

2, 7, 16, 20,
26, 31, 37, 41,
48, 52, 57, 63

My choices

Number	Suit	Choices by Suit/%

Register your results

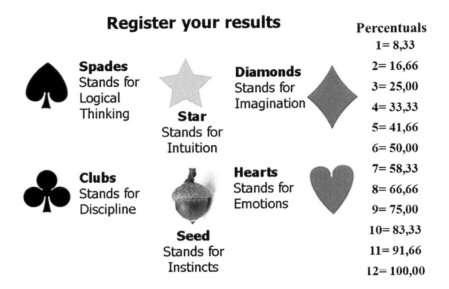

Spades
Stands for
Logical
Thinking

Star
Stands for
Intuition

Diamonds
Stands for
Imagination

Clubs
Stands for
Discipline

Seed
Stands for
Instincts

Hearts
Stands for
Emotions

Percentuals

1= 8,33
2= 16,66
3= 25,00
4= 33,33
5= 41,66
6= 50,00
7= 58,33
8= 66,66
9= 75,00
10= 83,33
11= 91,66
12= 100,00

Now you have your talent dominance profile: more than half (six or more cards) in a single suit feature a monodominant profile, whether in Star (spiritual), Spades (logical), Diamonds (creative), Clubs (methodical), Seed (visceral) or Hearts (romantic).

The monodominant profile is quite rare, describing persons stronger in a single skill pole than in the sum of all others. Among the more than 30,000 people(*) around the world who took the test you just took, less than 1,000 reached 75% or more of choices in a single of the six suits and, of these, not one in Star or Seed.

These surveys revealed that the most common talent profile is the tri-dominant, requiring the sum of a minimum of three suits to reach 75% (or more) of preferences. The second group is the bi-dominant, requiring the sum of two suits to reach those.

---

* Participants of "Brain Experience Meetings" carried out with business executives and leaders.

Figure 16.1 The four I's of apprenticeship

16

Whole Brain Teaching & Learning

In order to understand the learning process (and teaching, as a result), it is essential to understand how the mechanisms of reception and emission of the central nervous system of man and the peripheral mechanisms of this system work.

And also, to know how these systems evolved and evolve and how they behave differently from person to person.

Due to the differences in dominant brain polarity, the specific way in which each of us learn is peculiar. The specific way in which each one of us transmit, is peculiar, and the specific way in which each of us interpret what is transmitted and what is received is peculiar.

Each of us will learn better by knowing, understanding and managing our best reception and learning systems, while identifying, accessing and developing our secondary systems to build capacity on how to learn in a global and holistic way using all of our sensors.

Any teacher will teach better by identifying the receiving systems preferred by their pupils, while knowing, understanding and managing their best transmission systems (and feedback receiving), identifying, accessing and developing their secondary systems to learn to teach in a global and holistic way, using all its sensors and transmitters.

A very large number of educators around the world already recognize that this is so. However, many of them continue to advocate teaching recipes valid for all classes of audiences only to discover later that their recipes work wonderfully for some and are a fiasco for others. It is impossible to please everyone, especially those with clearly opposed skills such as "Greeks and Trojans".

Learning through the visceral pole is eminently tactile. Based on a remarkable individual experience in practice: fire burns, water wets, the dog bites.

It is knowledge endorsed by certainty. Certainty so strongly ingrained that it can pass (genetically?) from generation to generation, creating archetypes capable of dispensing practical individual experience.

Fear of heights is a good example. The child who has never fallen out of bed will not throw herself off the top of a piece of furniture on which she has been placed. Most likely she will protect herself, be scared and cry. In a way, she knows that she cannot fly and that the height is dangerous.

All subjects whose practice requires physical activity are partially or heavily learned through the visceral pole in the exact proportion of the physical component involved.

The most typical example is sporting activity of any grade. All sports, from the most instinctive ones such as running or jumping, include theoretical foundations learned through intellectual poles without which simple body training will be unable to produce the best results.

On the other hand, we know that it is impossible to form a champion simply through intellectual learning.

Driving a car, playing the piano or another musical instrument are also rich examples of the importance and value of body learning.

A typist or an experienced digitizer will know, with his eyes closed, when he touched the wrong key even if it is next to the one sought. His fingers already know where the different keys are.

Learning by doing reinforces the mastery of any discipline.

The biggest limitation of the organizational pole is its reduced holistic perception. Attentive to the details that can be seen with the eyes, he tends to lose the vision of the whole, at a spatial level, an important adjunct to the learning process.

Learning through the preventive/organizational (SW) pole is fundamentally visual, based on the observation of things and experiences lived or reported by others. The SW will learn better by seeing than by listening. For this reason, it is the reader par excellence, capturing and conserving information obtained through sequential texts and images, graphs and tables.

The SW is self-taught in the sense of having a superior ability to learn without interaction with a master. In fact, the master will only be well accepted by the SW if he transmits information sequentially, in an organized and orderly path, clean (with a paused and clear voice) and, preferably, supported by written texts, figures and explanatory gestures.

Abrupt or disconnected gestures of the transmitted information, dramatized vocal modulation, approach or physical contact will inhibit the apprehension of information by the SW.

In the same way, auditory reinforcement through recordings will only be useful if the restrictions regarding the "cleaning" of the text and the modulation of the voice are observed. Background music can help, whenever the rhythm is sequential and organized. Melodies that inspire or favor "travel" and ramblings will also inhibit the learning process through the SW.

Classrooms, as classically conceived, meet and fulfill (even without their creators consciously knowing) the organizational and discipline needs of the SW. The first teachers, however, were the SE and they taught with the pupils around them using their bodies and their voices.

The SW decided to organize the school. They placed all the desks in symmetrical rows, a huge blackboard in front and, amazing, a table with a chair for the teacher. Most teachers are still representatives of SE´s. They prefer to move around the room rather than occupy the post assigned to them.

Learning through the emotional/relational pole (SE) is essentially sensitive, based on the student's confidence and empathy with the teacher or the subject.

There is no effective learning at the SE pole without the figure of the teacher, fellow student or images and stories that touch the heart and feelings of the learner.

*Through his preventive/organizational
and emotional/relational skills, man moves
all of his conscious actions.
Therefore, the effective use of everything we
learn, essential to the consolidation of
acquired knowledge, depends crucially on these
skills.*

For this reason, he needs the support of paralanguage and will learn comfortably through sound recordings in which the speed, rhythm, modulation and intonation of the voice (music of language) are well explored.

Romantic music acts as a powerful adjunct to the SE learning process, as well as interactive activities with the group.

The kinesthetic learner (in the language of NLP) learns much better near the teacher (group organized in a circle) and feels discomfort in a traditional classroom, particularly if placed in the back rows, away from the teacher.

In this situation, he will try to interact with his colleagues during classes, being frequently taken for undisciplined.

Fortunately, many teachers tend to call the "undisciplined" for their first portfolios. Unfortunately, these same teachers will try to inhibit their interactions and cause their isolation from colleagues and self.

Isolation can even neutralize the kinesthetic's ability to learn. That is why he will always prefer cinema to television (unless watched in groups). Its self-taught aptitude can be explored in cinema or with visits to exhibitions, museums and fairs.

His aptitude for studying technical texts in books is very low, although he is an excellent reader of poetry and novels.

Learning through the analytical/factual (NW) pole is fundamentally architectural, built geometrically on the assessment and analysis of facts and data placed more visually than auditorily.

Figures or images must portray reality.

Metaphors or concept illustrations show low credibility for NW.

Likewise, emotion-laden information is uncomfortable and unreliable for its view.

Demonstrations, tests and practical experiences are essential for the NW´s apprenticeship process, because the reasoning of NW is critical par excellence, prone to doubting what he has not found.

Appeals to his imagination do not work. Not because he doesn't know how to imagine, but because he doesn't trust that criterion.

The NW only speculates through practical experience and never spatially. This means that the hypotheses he formulates move one by one or in groups (test the hypotheses before generating others).

Many great inventors were prominent representatives of dominance at the NW pole. But they were not really inventors, but discoverers. The inventors or creators are representatives of the NE pole.

The close or interacting teacher introduces noise into the NW learning process. He can study in groups and get excellent results from it whenever the relationship between the group members is particularly cold, formal and objective, without social ramblings. Music, as an adjunct, is less significant and will be counterproductive if romantic, restless or fanciful.

Still learning through the intuitive/conceptual pole (NE) is eminently holistic and speculative. Information is captured through written or spoken language and, particularly, through metaphorical images, figures or illustrations representing ideas or concepts, rather than things in themselves.

The NE is not interested in details, but in the overall picture. He has the need to process the information he receives by "walking" his imagination around them.

For this reason, the presence of a sequential instructor speaking without interruption on any subject will introduce noise into his learning process. When he catches an idea, reading or listening, he will immediately tend to start a journey around it for the establishment of global interrelations.

Whenever a section read contains information worthy of processing, he will interrupt the reading, close the eyes and keeps on thinking about it for a few moments or for a long time, before resuming reading.

Under these conditions, live instruction will tend to be deficient for the NE. When he hears information he wants to process, his intentions may be interrupted or hindered by the continuation of the lecture. Although he is an essentially auditory learner (he closes his eyes to understand and learns in greater depth what he hears), the live performances may turn to be irritating to him.

Unless having an instructor fully attuned to his learning process, the NE will learn better and much faster on his own, becoming a self-taught par excellence.

Music, especially that capable of inducing imaginative "journeys", multiplies his capacity for learning.

Right at birth and during the first months and years of its life, the child is more able than ever to receive all the learning that can flow through the visceral and emotional systems. On the day of birth, the baby can learn to swim without any difficulty. In the same way, it will be easier for one to start developing all their body skills.

By observing the sequence of development of brain skills from the bottom up, parents will know exactly what and how to teach preschoolers.

This is the best time to guide their children´s emotions.

After the age of eight until long after reaching adulthood and maturity, man's intellectual development will still find plenty of room for progress. His emotional development however will be almost fatally compromised, for better or for worse.

Parents who hope that children can understand things in order to start to more accurately parameterize their education have already missed the train.

More than that, it should be remembered that the visceral nature of learning in early childhood ensures that teaching supported by physical stimuli, both in terms of punishment and reward, works as well as in the training of animals.

*The most elementary and vital things
that man has learned throughout
his evolution are stored
in the Corporal/Visceral pole.
As much as he develops as a rational being
and thinking, he will continue to learn
through his visceral skills.
And he will not forget the things that he
learned through that pole.*

17

Communication and Negotiation

While communication and negotiation are the specialties of the emotional/relational pole (SE), all brain skills are involved in these processes.

The intuitive/conceptual (NE) suggests the possible interest in establishing a relationship not compelled by emotional levers.

The analytical/factual (NW) seeks data and facts that confirm this interest to complete the diagnosis of the opportunity, make a decision and establish the logical and rational objectives of the negotiation.

The preventive/organizational (SW) organizes this information and plans the approach in order to guarantee its success, protect itself against eventual failures and plan contingency actions to minimize the effects of one eventual failure.

The emotional/relational (SE) adjusts the system of representation of the issuer or negotiator to the system preferred by the interlocutor and provides the opening of "tuning" in the negotiation process.

Seems complicated? Let's put it in a colloquial language: the goal of effective communication is to promote the understanding and acceptance of ideas and proposals.

Many people understand by communication the simple act of issuing a message (an announcement) verbally or in writing.

This perspective is certainly a result of the fad published by the media, associating the idea of a communicator with people who talk non-stop.

However, communication is a circular process that begins with the emission of a message and is only completed when it produces a positive response, embodied in the actions of the message recipients going through the reception processes (listening, seeing, feeling), understanding, approval and positive response.

There is no communication activity that does not seek a positive response. Even the sports announcer, who simply narrates the moves of a football match, has the objective of being approved by the listener and get his positive reaction, formalized in the decision to listen again, through that station, to the next broadcasts.

This applies clearer and fuller to all auditorium animators, who seem concerned only with spitting out information.

If you speak and the intended recipient does not hear, there is no communication.

If he hears but does not understand, there is no communication.

If he understands but does not agree, your communication goal has not been achieved.

If he agrees, but does not do what you intended him to do, the communication is unsuccessful.

Therefore, to ensure the success of communication, it is not enough to activate the typical faculties of the SE pole.

It is essential to have, first of all, a global and ideal vision of your goals, provided through the skills of the intuitive /conceptual pole (NE).

Then, ensure that this view is as realistic as possible, through its rational critique of the analytical/factual (NW) pole.

These two steps account for the process of establishing your goals in the communication or negotiation process.

If you don't know what your goal is in the communication process, you won't know if and when it was achieved. Whether you were successful or not.

Once you have established a destination or goal, it's easier to plan a travel itinerary – an action plan to achieve your goal.

Predicting and planning the initiatives and actions to be undertaken to ensure the success of each communication and negotiation process, preparing the environment, organizing your information, taking up your weapons and going on a mission are tasks that imply activating the typical skills of the SW pole.

Thereafter, the communicator or negotiator will take action. But if everything that has been done up to that point has not taken into account the interlocutor's perceptions, truths and emotions, his brain dominance and his preferred representation systems, the communicator can go completely wrong.

People with dominant skills very prominent in any of the skill poles will find it easy to communicate with people of similar level of fitness in the same pole (NW with NW – digital; NE with NE – auditory; SW with SW – visual; SE with SE – kinesthetic) both because they use the same representation systems and have many aptitudes, skills and interests in common.

Communication and understanding between two or more individuals with dominant skills in neighboring poles in the same cerebral hemisphere (right or left) NW with SW or NE with SE implies a certain level of difficulty, which can be overcome through the various interests they have in common.

Greater difficulty is found in communication and understanding between individuals with dominant skills in neighboring poles located in opposite cerebral hemispheres (left and right): NW with NE or SW with SE, because their perspective, values and systems of representation are very different.

People with skills dominance in opposite brain hemispheres have small interests in common and can only communicate efficiently through concessions, from both sides, characterized by the use, in the negotiation process, of their non-dominant skills: one or the other using values and representation systems consistent with the pole of dominance and the representation system of their interlocutor.

The greatest potential difficulty inherent in the communications process lies in the fact that each of us is, strictly and systematically, attached to his own ideas. "In each head a sentence" has become a universal perception.

This is natural and human, but communication between people will be blocked if they are not prepared or willing to open concessions.

Extreme difficulty occurs in communication between individuals with dominant skills in diametrically opposite poles: non-neighbors and belonging to different hemispheres (SW with NE or SE with NW).

In these cases, their interests, points of view and representation systems are often conflicting and the willingness of one or the other to use poles of skills similar to those of their interlocutor is impaired. Probably none of them will want to open concessions, hoping that the other will do it first.

Observe this phenomenon in the analysis of a real dialogue between the commercial director of a company (Raul) and its managing director (Claude):

Commercial Director: – Mr. Claude, every time we analyze the need to boost our business, we consider a proposal or two and, if they are not approved, we run out of alternatives and end up doing nothing!

Superintendent and Production Director: – Doing Nothing?

(CD) – In a meeting of professionals in which I participated last week, we came across a list of sixty possible measures to boost the business of a company that is not very different from ours. I understand that, analyzing this list, we can find some that apply well to our case.

(SD) – Provisions in the sales area ?!

(CD) – In all areas. Production, technology...

(SD) – All the arrangements in the production area have already been completed!

(CD) – Mr. Claude, the only thing we did in the production area was to double the work shift. We have done nothing to improve quality or productivity and the fact is that there are at least ten vectors to be analyzed to arrive at an adequate assessment of our industrial productivity.

(SD) – Ten vectors ?!

(SD) – Exactly. Examine this instrument (hand over a form).

(SD Looking at the document with visible ill will)

– I already have many things to worry about, don't come to fill my head with junk! (Returns the form).

* * *

Raul, the commercial director, had clearly defined in his mind a proposal capable of, without major cost implications, improving production and productivity, but what Claude heard was a proposal for him to work harder, permeated by the hint that he was not doing his job well.

Overcoming this type of communication difficulty depends, basically, on the initiative of the issuer – the individual who triggers the process – through the search for harmony with his interlocutor.

The aim of "tuning" is to eliminate noise of any kind in the communication process: to make communication clear and limpid.

This is possible when the sender, before opening his ideas, points of view and preferred representation system, observes his interlocutor and tries to gain access to his ideas, points of view and preferred representation system, in order to locate initial contact points or area of interest and common ground.

He can do this with ease, recognizing and valuing the positions of his interlocutor (planting reciprocity) and getting closer to the interlocutor representation system:

(CD, looking for harmony) – Mr. Claude, I have been following your work with production and I feel that your main concern has been to attend sales quickly.

(SD) – Now I want to see if you can sell more, as always proposed.

(SD) – With the action you took to double the production shift, we will be able to encourage real sales! Will this second round cost too much?

(SD) – If we have more revenue, it will pay off.

(CD) – That's right. Production costs always end up increasing. Wouldn't it be nice if we could also have gains on production costs?

(SD) – It would be great, but I'm doing everything I can.

(CD) – Are you satisfied with the product/man/ hour ratio?

(SD) – No. I think these guys are slow, but it is difficult to find specialized people.

(DC) – Like who, for example?

(SD) – Like Peter, George... the old class.

(CD) – Well though. If we had several Peters and Georges, how many units do you think we could manage per man /hour?

(SD) – Much more!

(CD) – And with higher quality too? And more material savings?

(SD) – Yes! It would be a great deal.

(CD) – From what I am feeling, is the quality of the workforce your main concern?

(SD) – Without a doubt! This is where we would solve our problems.

(CD) – Wouldn't it be interesting if we could build a standard team with the old ones, in a position to teach and serve as a model for the others?

(SD) – It seems like an excellent idea!

* * *

In this second version, Raul got in tune with Claude using his own relational skills and communication resources at the kinesthetic level.

It is not a matter of concealing his ideas or points of view or pretending that he believes in things that he does not believe. Both Claude and Raul have skills and perceptions in all poles of dominance, although their dominant systems are different. For this reason, Raul, who feels the need to communicate efficiently with Claude, takes the initiative to use, at that moment, his kinesthetic system.

* * *

It would be wrong to pretend that Claud, in addition to adhering to his proposal and his views, also adhered to his preferred representation system (in the original case, the digital, opposite to the kinesthetic).

This is a golden rule for interpersonal communication and negotiation processes: "If you want to get someone's interest and support for your points of view, place them in a way that the other is able to understand and accept."

Dale Carnegie, more than half a century ago, in his bestseller How to Make Friends and Influence People, stated: *"If you want someone to be interested in you, start by becoming interested in him"*.

In scientific language, derived from the analysis of brain skills and preferred communication systems (NLP), we can say: "If you want someone to be in tune with you, start by getting in tune with him".

In Chapter 26, you will find proposals for the exercises you should do to increase your ability to communicate more effectively with people of different poles of dominant brain skills and preferred communication systems.

Train to do this and in a short time you will become a master in this art.

Rarely has any text or training program in the areas of negotiation and sales failed to emphasize the importance of the tuning process.

However, most of them have failed to draw attention to the fact that successful behaviors in this area cannot be simply rehearsed and mechanically practiced.

Anyone of average intelligence will be able to distinguish authenticity from falsehood. And nobody likes to be manipulated.

The understanding and appreciation of individual differences inherent to the phenomenon of cerebral multipolarity have their greatest strength in the process of allowing you to build a real and sincere interest in people by developing attitudes that will be expressed in sincere and spontaneous behaviors.

Thus, getting in tune with your interlocutors will never be a trick, but, above all, a natural and inherent procedure to the correct and expected social performance of all individuals.

Body language and paralanguage are more reliable than verbal language because they are much older and ingrained communication systems in the human mind.

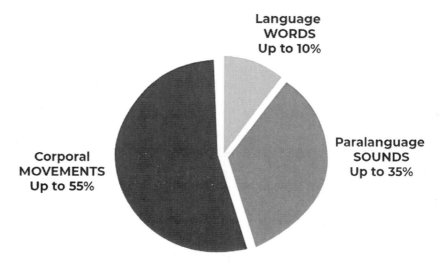

Figure 17.1 Reability of representational systems

***When each member of a team
is commited to support the others
and meet their needs
everyone will be supported
and have their own needs met.***

18

Whole Brain Team Work

The performance of working in teams, whether in meetings or in the daily routine, is negatively affected by the diversified perceptions that people have about the different situations and problems to be faced.

In fact, the dominant brain skill differences, with all their consequences on environmental reading optics (windows) and preferred representation systems (NLP), are the root behind most communication and understanding difficulties among members of any team.

While oblivious to this problem, we recognize as our paradigms of vision and interpretation of all phenomena our particular way of understanding these phenomena. As a consequence, all views and interpretations different from ours seem erroneous, short-sighted, or malicious.

As soon as we have the opportunity to know, appreciate and understand the phenomenon of cerebral multipolarity, we realize that there is no right or wrong in the processes of environmental analysis and communications. We understand that each human being is unique and distinct from the others and that his way of interpreting environmental phenomena, people's behaviors and the messages he receives is the only one that makes sense to him.

Self-control and piety pointed out as two key components of "Emotional Intelligence" are characteristic abilities of the lower brain poles described in the "Cerebral Multipolarity" model.

This perception leads us, immediately, to review our concepts about the "right way" or the "wrong way" to see the world and people. And also, to realize that our differences, instead of creating problems of understanding between us, can be capitalized on profitable synergy.

We started to realize the value of symbiosis and to understand the old popular sayings, which state things like: "two boll weeds don't kiss", "opposites attract", "in each head a sentence".

Self-control is one of the most typical skills of the preventive/organizational pole (SW). Piety is one of the most typical skills of the emotional/relational pole (SE), responsible for the abilities to read the emotions of others, for empathy and altruism.

Controlling your own emotions is essential for you to be in tune with others emotions.

The process of maximizing synergy in planning and action begins with the full opening of the mind to individual differences, both at the intellectual levels (diagnosis) and at the operational or emotional levels (actions).

When you understand and value the way you see the world, at the same time that you understand and value the way others see the world, the basic conditions are created for the full alignment of minds and hearts, essential to maximize work performance in a team.

This alignment, of course, has to be provided through clear and open exposition about how each member of the group sees and interprets different situations.

If you do not know what the other person thinks about a particular situation, you cannot start a process of understanding with him, even if you are open-minded to accept interpretations different from yours. The reverse is also true. A real case can elucidate this aspect well.

At a recent meeting, we had just identified the different brain skills of the participants noting that the group had both dominantly emotional (SE) and deeply rational (NE) people.

At a certain point in the meeting, after making a series of statements, I had to leave immediately, for no more than two minutes.

When I returned, the atmosphere was frankly in turmoil with people arguing heatedly.

Trying to find out what the issue was, I heard from the "factual":

– You said such and such... but that is not a fact!

I asked:

– Could you put your doubt in a relational language?

Reasoning in a fraction of a second, he replied:

– What did you mean with your statement before leaving?

And he heard my clarification murmuring: Ah... I understand.

The discussion stopped immediately making it

clear to everyone that they were heated debating a statement that just hadn't been clearly understood by anyone.

This is how group communication flows outside the understanding of the processes of attunement among group participants.

From the moment this harmony is established, communication barriers are broken and bridges are created for the exchange of views and concepts interpreted within the dominant systems of each participant.

From then on, the optimization of teamwork results depends on the objective placement and distribution of the roles to be played by each participant uppon the perception of their interdependence as "suppliers" and "customers" of each other along a chain of processes, and the understanding by suppliers of the specific needs and demands of their clients, and the performance of individual tasks capable of ensuring that these needs are met in a timely manner.

This means, in a nutshell, that team members will be working effectively to ensure that each of them helps the others to complete their tasks and accomplish their goals.

In practice, this behavior corresponds to the inversion of the extremely common process in team environments when each is simply waiting for the other to provide the necessary support to complement their tasks and meet their needs.

Reciprocity is the key to success in teamwork and, if you are simply waiting for your interlocutor to take the initiative to do what you need, the best reciprocity you can hope for is for them to simply wait for you to take the initiative to do what he needs.

Go ahead and take the initiative in the process using your communication and negotiation skills to inform, convince, motivate and get positive responses from your colleagues.

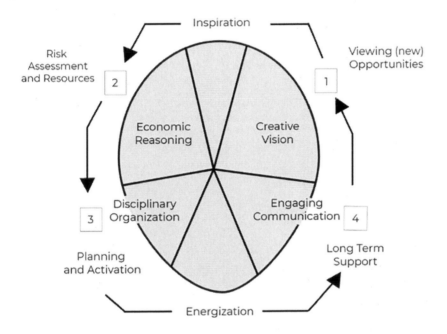

Figure 18.1 Whole Brain Team Work

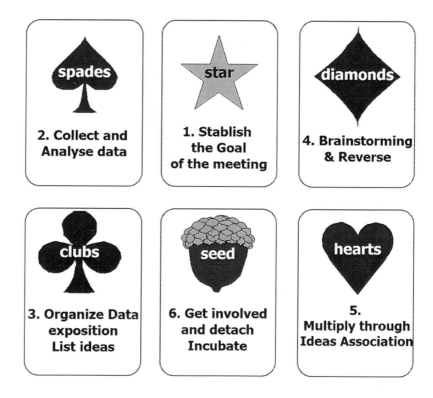

Figure 19.1 Whole Brain Creative Process

19

Whole Brain Creative Process

The creativity seen only as the ability to imagine and generate hypotheses for understanding or solving problems is closely related to the skills contained in the intuitive/conceptual pole (NE) of the human brain.

However, the creative process, capable of generating useful and optimized diagnoses and responses for any kind of human problems and needs, in life and at work, involves the entire set of brain skills including formal logical reasoning, typical of the NW pole, and the organizational preventive reasoning, typical of the SW pole, which, strictly speaking, would be the most conservative, resistant and even averse to the continuous development of new hypotheses and ideas.

The multipolar creative process capable of leading to useful and effective discoveries, inventions and innovations begins with the definition and clear understanding of the problem or situation being addressed. This requires the activation of formal logical reasoning, charged with seeking and collecting all available data and facts, essential to the study and real knowledge of the different situations focused on.

Even the most speculative and creative spirit needs to work on a database of facts.

This does not mean that impressions or opinions

cannot be used to solve a given problem, but that we must be ready to abandon any hypotheses that we have raised if we encounter facts that are contrary to them.

The organizational sense participates in the creative process ordering and sequencing information and imponng discipline for the approach course, especially when creative work is performed in groups.

Relational biases or communication skills are called upon to interfere in the creative process for integration of the participants in the process, maximizing group synergy, and also to assure that, whether in individual work or in teamwork, the human side of all situations will be taken into account ("How will people accept or react to this idea?").

Pure imagination, speculation and creativity return to the scene to provide the generation of quantities of ideas through the process of stirring ideas or "brainstorming".

At that moment, what matters the most is to separate creation and judgment in time.

First, just create, without concern for quality. Later, judge the ideas generated and look for quality.

A new round of activation of the skills of each pole begins with the convocation of logical reasoning for sections of consideration, evaluation and criticism of the ideas originaly generated under the aegis of the total absence of judgment and even for the free "graffiti" of all the ideas that came up (reverse brainstorming).

The organizational sense is envited to sequence and review the proposals and contents placed until that moment preparing the triggering of the period for incubation

The incubation process that has along times given rise to the emergence of great discoveries and inventions is, in reality, the effort to send ideas and judgments consciously generated to mix with information housed in the subconscious and even unconscious levels of the mind.

Visceral and spiritual potentials (S and N) will have then the opportunity to interfere in the process to offer real enlightenment.

But this rarely and only incidentally happens. What creators often call enlightenment is just a conscious or emotional decision in favor of the idea that looks brilliant.

The success in implementing the response found as a result of the creative process will depend, crucially, on the commitment to it by the people or groups involved.

The process of using all brain skills in creation is important because the goal of creativity cannot be to generate any response to address opportunities or problems. What is always sought is the best answer capable of generating maximum results with minimum effort for full implementation.

Therefore, individuals or members of interested groups must visualize the best idea (using NE), evaluate concretely its potential effectiveness and organize (using SW) its rigorous implementation and, above all, falling in love with the idea and assuming full commitment with its success.

For this final stage, the typical skills of the SE pole are activated again and sustained "*without question or pause.*"(*)

In view of these demands of the creative process, it

---

* *"The Impossible Dream" (song by Joe Darion & Mitch Leigh)*

is clear that the best composition for a working group interested in proposals development and generation of new ideas, capable of working in practice and giving the expected result, is not the meeting of the "most creative", but the composition of different skills involved (creative, practical, clean and exciting).

To a social columnist, famous in the 60s, is attributed the statement that *"all unanimity is stupid"*.

In the light of cerebral multipolarity, unanimity (among people of the same cerebral dominance) is not stupid, but, certainly, short sighted.

For this reason, the potentially useful creative process can benefit greatly from the assembly of heterogeneous groups, by heterogeneity being understood not simply the designation of people with different knowledge, but, above all, people with different ways of thinking and seeing the world.

20

Whole Brain Business Management

All the sciences, all the arts and all the technologies derived from them, including business management, were generated by the skills contained in the oldest and most sophisticated device at the service of man: his brain.

However, as the subsidiary sciences, disciplines and technologies began to devote themselves, man, with increasing frequency, began to make decisions and take actions based exclusively on specific teachings contained in each discipline. As the exact, human and biological sciences have distinct and separate paths, this tendency to adhere to the disciplines has given rise to increasingly sectorial and narrow-minded proposals that restrict the use of the intellectual and operational skills of individuals and groups in their fullness.

The most notable consequence of these "disciplinary" approaches to business management has been the generation of various types of organizational myopia and an endless back and forth of fads in all areas of business administration, with the exacerbated growth of the lucrative "gurus" industry of administration.

To avoid being at the mercy of fads, it is necessary

to use more intelligence and less gurus, no matter how much one can and should take advantage of their teachings.

There is an intimate and obvious relationship between cerebral multipolarity and organizational subsystems for the simple fact that the latter organizational subsystems have their origin precisely in the differences in brain dominance among men, taken to the business scenarion.

- The information/decision subsystem relates to the NE pole (intuitive-conceptual) skills.
- The technical/economic subsystem relates to the skills of the NW (analytical-factual) pole.
- The administrative/structural subsystem relates to the skills of the SW pole (preventive-organizational) and the human/social sub-system relates to the skills of the SE pole (emotional-relational).

The recognition of these facts bring contributions of extraordinary value, not only to the understanding of many basic phenomena of business management, but, particularly, to the conscious and programmed administration of these phenomena.

We refer, in particular, to the fundamental challenges of the context that begins with the formulation of the business vision of any company until the effective implementation of all measures capable of transforming that vision into concrete achievements.

Often, the business vision is formulated in a typical "language" of the intuitive/conceptual pole, rather than in an analytical/factual language.

As such, it rarely makes sense from a "rational" perspective.

Therefore, the process of taking the vision into action begins with the statement of the vision and business strategies in different forms, all of them making clear sense for each of the poles of brain dominance.

It has to be placed in formulas and numbers for NW, in sequential charts or graphs for the SW and in the form of proposals that value the human element and its relationships for the SE.

This means that the company's business vision and strategies, in order to be well assumed by all, need to be anchored in all poles of brain dominance.

The same happens with technological projects, economic plans and budgets generated in the technical/economic subsystem, under the control of analytical current reasoning (NW), and with operational plans, execution schedules, performance manuals and means of control generated in administrative subsystem, under the control of preventive/organizational (SW) reasoning.

In contrast, the proposals for motivation, leadership, continuing education and empowerment generated in the human/social sub-system, under the control of emotional/relational reasoning (SE), have to be well "sold" within other sub-systems where they often smell like perfumery.

Only in this way we will arrive at a company within which all reasoning and behavior subsystems are perfectly aligned with the proposal for the full use of brain skills to optimize management.

Throughout the world, the perception that successful companies and professionals have grounded and will ground, increasingly, their performance on three essential skills:

1. Diagnosis: Ability to look, see and understand, including the concern to continuously monitor the environment around the company and the internal environment, in order to identify, in time, opportunities, threats and problems, their understanding and decision making about them (what to do).

2. Adaptation: Ability to adjust knowledge, attitudes, behaviors and everything else that can be under control to the contingencies of the different diagnosed situations, mobilizing and organizing resources for the quick and effective reaction to threats, occupation of opportunities and solution of problems.

3. Communication: Ability to implement and sustain projects by effectively communicating its goals and proposals to achieve the adhesion, contribution and commitment of employees, suppliers and customers, generating and sustaining partnership relationships at work and in business.

These skills are contained, respectively, in NW and NE (diagnosis), SW (adaptation) and SE (communication) brain poles, being evident the decisive executive participation of the lower brain poles in the process of effective approach, implementation and support of all measures at work.

The cerebral cortex mainly thinks, while the limbic system mainly moves actions and reactions.

The set of preventive/organizational and emotional/ relational skills, contained in the lower brain poles SW and SE, comprise the "operating system" of the human mind (the abilities detached within the concept of emotional intelligence).

It is through this system that we put into action all decisions resulting from the diagnostic processes developed by the intellectual inclinations of the upper cerebral hemisphere.

It is for no other reason that the value of emotional intelligence at work is emphasized.

Still, it must be evident that success in business management cannot rely solely on action.

Modern business management is based on seven pillars or sequential functions involving (*):

1. Orientation: Formal strategic positioning of the company containing the outlines of its business vision (destination and course), permanent and macro-objective guidelines.

2. Information: Data capture and information processing system, in all areas, to feed the decision-making and management process along these seven pillars.

3. Planning: Deployment of the decision and strategic guidance in terms of operational objectives containing the description of the ways, means and deadlines for achieving them, as well as budgets, instruments and relevant control procedures.

4. Organization: Mobilization of resources (natural, human and physical-financial) so that planning can be carried out with maximum effectiveness and efficiency.

5. Communications: Exchange of information and interpersonal and interdepartmental coordination to ensure the fluency of processes involving the participation of different departments and people.

6. Motivation: Provision of appropriate actions to move the processes of awareness, involvement and commitment required at all levels.

7. Leadership: Activation, monitoring and control of all processes triggered; and promotion of continuous and progressive training of all people involved.

*Back to 1995 we have paraphrased
the work of T.E. Lawrence
(Lawrence of Arabia) baptizing this sequence as
"Seven Pillars of (Managerial) Wisdom".*

Analyzing these functions closely under the light of the concepts of Multipolar Intelligence it becomes evident that they are sequentially linked to the brain skills of the NE, NW, SW and SE poles, with the former at the intellectual level and the latter at the operational and emotional levels.

The assessment of the performance level of these functions in several large first-rate companies has clearly shown that some see themselves or are stronger in intellectual system while others see themselves or are stronger in operating/emotional system.

In any case, executives involved in these evaluations, even without having any information on the issues raised by cerebral multipolarity, realize the need to equalize the performance of all these functions to ensure the continued success and the optimization of the company's results.

They recognize the importance of using brain skills to the full in business management.

21

The Entrepreneurial Process

The instruments for assessing dominant brain skills applied by The Ned Herrmann Group to more than 1,000 entrepreneurs, in the United States and around the world, revealed that more than 70% have a predominantly experimental profile (corresponding, in the Ned Herrmann model, to the NE pole).

The first idea that derives from this observation is that the typical entrepreneur is an individual with strong intuitive/conceptual inclinations.

There is no way to deny this, mainly because the first step in the entrepreneurial process often implies a willingness to try, to experiment, to take the risk.

However, it is good to know that, worldwide, more than half of all new products, new ideas and new businesses launched each year do not complete one year of life. Among the survivors, another half do not reach the third year.

And the most frequent reason behind these failures has been undercapitalization – entrepreneurs did not have the bankroll to fund their initiatives.

Second, marketing errors appear starting with the characterization of the business opportunity or the idea itself: the entrepreneur's vision was not supported by the real needs or interests of the market.

In any case, it appears that the entrepreneur lacked a critical sense to evaluate his ideas in the light of the facts. There was no "bridge" between fantasy and reality.

The long-term successful entrepreneurial process develops over four subsequent and continuous steps:

1. Visualization of a business opportunity.
2. Concrete assessment of inherent risks and resources.
3. Planning and activating of ideal action.
4. Long-term support.

This process is natural and spontaneous because it is guided by the different brain skills of all human beings and a curious and very illustrative reference to this can be found in an excerpt from the major work of the Nobel Prize for literature, Gabriel García Márquez, "One Hundred Years of Solitude", first published in 1967 when no work on such brain skills had been made public:

"Aureliano conceived the craziest projects as immediate possibilities. Made rational calculations about costs and time and carried them out with no exasperation brakes".

In this paragraph, García Márquez describes, with precision and wonderful power of synthesis, the typical behaviors of a person using sequentially the skills of the conceptual, factual, organizational and relational poles.

It is a magical description of the entrepreneurial

process, learned through the simple observation of successful entrepreneurs who would have inspired the elaboration of the Aureliano's profile.

Well noted. The successful entrepreneurial process is, in effect, the sequential activation of the individual's natural aptitudes. Analyzing these skills in the light of cerebral multipolarity, we will find, in the sequence NE-N-NW-SW-S-SE, the following personal qualities:

1. Creative vision
2. Inspiration
3. Economic reasoning
4. Disciplinary organization
5. Emotional energy
6. Engaging communication.

What is your strongest point? And the weakest?

If you're one SW par excellence, you probably won't be interested in launching yourself as one entrepreneur, unless you're so confident in what you're doing is in the shadow of any risk; that you can do better than the company you work for now and don't feel the slightest need to keep your current job because you have, for instance, a lot of cash savings.

If you are one NE par excellence, you will probably start to design another business before executing the idea you now have in mind.

In any other case, you can access, use and develop all the necessary skills, whether or not they are your dominant skills.

See how the spontaneous entrepreneurial process occurs:

- Using the aptitudes characteristic of the conceptual pole (NE), the entrepreneur visualizes, in the environment, what appears to be an opportunity and conceives its occupation.
- Appealing to the faculties of the factual pole (NW), he gathers data and information about the perceived situation, analyzes and evaluates the opportunity and costs involved and makes a decision about it.
- Accessing the capacities of the organizational pole (SW) plans its actions, orders them in time and space and establishes the essential measures for course control, protection (planning to avoid deviations) and contingency (what to do if the initial steps fail), mobilize the necessary resources and take action.
- From then on, he will persistently move (without exasperation breaks) his relationship skills (SE) to achieve the adhesion and commitment of all those on whom the success of his enterprise depends (employees, suppliers and customers).

Failures to use any of these skills can take you to the crossroads of failure encountered by most entrepreneurs:

- The entrepreneur sees what appears to be an opportunity and immediately starts moving to occupy it, without dwelling on a broader survey of the set of opportunities in the environment and without paying attention to the threats also present in the environment, going over the phases of evaluation and planning.

- The analysis and evaluation phase is conducted without any technical rigor and the impressions and opinions end up prevailing over the data and facts.

- Assessment to opportunity is poorly designed and poorly planned. Budgets, schedules and flows of activities are not even thought or proposed. Control means are not incorporated into the planning, which is left without protection and contingency.

- Well-engineered ideas and carefully elaborated plans are wrecked by deficient installation or long-term support. The parties involved are not properly instructed, trained or motivated to commit to results, and when things get tough, the first impulse is to abandon the project or give up on its goals.

The process of making full use of your brain skills in management is the only concrete way to overcome these crossroads.

This process, which we call Whole Brain Entrepreneurship, is justified and explored in more detail as follows.

The successful manager of companies in the third millennium will be the one who is able to access and use all their brain skills: creativity, logic, organization and communication, whether they are dominant or not, in a continuous and alternating emphasis process.

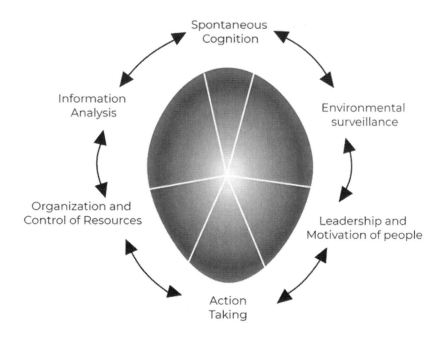

Figure 21.1 The Intrepreneurial Process

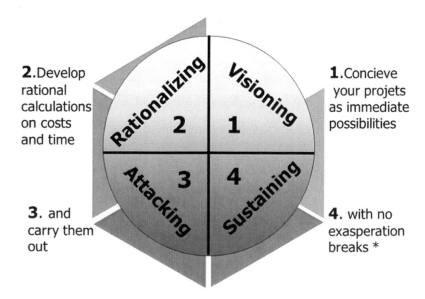

Figure 21.2 The E-FACTOR in 4 steps

22

Whole Brain Entrepreneurship

The analysis of the entrepreneurial process allows us to elaborate a deep assessment of the management process in all its connotations, based on the classic conception of the managerial function.

Classic business literature refers to the manager's role as planning, organizing and controlling (POC) or planning, organizing, leading and controlling (POLC).

Within this perspective, the skills requested from the manager would be, basically, those contained in the preventive/organizational pole (SW).

However, it is evident that, before planning, the manager needs to obtain information about the situations he must manage and then make decisions about it.

These functions related to the dynamics of looking, seeing and understanding different situations (diagnosing) and assuming a position in front of them (deciding) involve, by their nature, skills and processes quite different from those required in the planning function. They require intuitive/conceptual (NE) and analytical/factual (NW) skills.

It is also evident that most of the managers' time is not spent on planning and organizing work, but on active control activities (keeping track and avoiding deviations), guidance and leadership of subordinates and an uninterrupted exchange of information (communication) with peers, superiors and third parties, which are typical of the emotional /relational (SE) area.

A complete view of the scope of management activity will cover the functions of:

1. Environmental monitoring: To identify external or internal situations that require management: opportunities to be taken advantage of, threats to be avoided or problems to be solved.

2. Analysis and evaluation: Detailed study of situations, gathering of data and information, quantification, criticism, diagnosis and decision to approach (what to do).

3. Attack or access: Generating responses to diagnosed situations (how to do it). Planning of actions, means and control systems, prevention of deviations, protection and contingency. Organization (mobilization of resources and people) and administration.

4. Implementation and support: involvement, commitment and activation of people, persuasion, overcoming resistance, coordination, active leadership, training, competence building and empowerment.

As each manager prizes more or less each of these activities, they can be clearly perceived in the light of cerebral multipolarity:

- The most intuitive, abstract, speculative and holistic (NE) will have a greater inclination towards environmental monitoring activities.
- The most logical, concrete, numerical and

detailed (NW) will have a greater inclination towards the activities of analysis and evaluation of concrete phenomena.

- The most methodical, careful, disciplined and administrative (SW) will have a greater inclination towards activities to access or attack already established situations.
- The most romantic, expressive, sensitive and poetic (SE) will have a greater inclination towards the activities of orientation, involvement and training of people.

When managing the work of others, these individuals will vent their dominant characteristics, moving different focuses of management.

The classic view of the POC manager gives prestige to the management characterized by administrative skills (SW).

Therefore, this was the sovereign management paradigm, in effect until the 1960s.

The technological boom of the 1970s brought about a new bifocal (or bipolar) management paradigm with the growth of interest in technological skills (NW). The emergence of participative management, in the 1980s, proposed a new bifocal paradigm, honoring relational skills (SE).

The environmental turbulence characteristic of the 90s and 21st century is giving strength to a new bifocal paradigm, honoring creativity and visionary skills (NE).

But it is easy to see that the enrichment of work and management calls, above all, for a multifocal approach (Figure 23.1) where all skills are on the scene and in a continuous shift of emphasis.

Use imagination and creativity to see beyond appearances and focus on new and more complex situations, which require multiple and innovative responses.

Use logical and formal reasoning for a complete analysis of facts and available data and absorption of lived experiences.

Plan, organize and strictly control all business actions, keeping the defensive reasoning, typical of the SW pole, to face abrupt changes.

Make the most of relational skills to manage all communication and human relationship problems and, above all, develop people.

To achieve these purposes, it is up to managers, entrepreneurs and business leaders to exercise the development of all their brain skills towards a new paradigm of full (whole brain) management, more effective and efficient in all situations and opportunities.

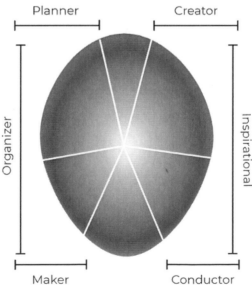

Figure 23.1 Leader Stiles typic of diverse Brain Dominances

23

Leadership Profiles

Dominant skills have a marked influence on people's behavior in leading subordinates and dependents. Psychology and management had already cataloged different behavioral profiles in business leaders without being able to safely establish the logic of these behaviors.

In light of cerebral multipolarity, these behaviors can be more than explained, predicted (Figure 23.1).

Leaders with dominant skills in the NW pole will take care, as a priority, on determine what and how should be done, creating ready responses for the work of the subordinates (planner leader).

Those with dominant skills in the SW pole will devote their best attention to following the rules and routines for controlling ongoing processes (controlling leader).

Those with dominant skills in the SW and S poles will be urged to "get their hands dirty" and do the job of subordinates, hoping only that they will imitate them without the possibility of doing better (maker leader).

Those with dominant skills in the S and SE poles, on the other hand, will tend to help their subordinates to do the job, staying by their side and trying to unite the group into a synergistic whole (conductor leader).

Those with dominant skills in the SE pole will try to guide and inspire their subordinates so that they grow and gain competence in their work, freeing themselves from the routines for carrying out a more creative work (inspirational leader).

Finally, those with dominant NE pole skills will find it more correct to focus primarily on creating new ways of doing things, without worrying about subordinates as people (creator leader).

One of the most important contributions of the Situational Leadership Theory, developed by Paul Hersey and Kenneth Blanchard, was to draw attention to the fact that there is not and cannot be a single ideal style of leadership or, consequently, a rigid pattern of behavior for the ideal leader.

Some leaders believe more in an authoritarian and directive standard, others defend a frankly democratic and participative management. Most are in the middle.

Situational leadership has proposed – and thus has become the most successful model in the world – that the leader is ideal behavior cannot depend on his beliefs or personality, but on the specific situation faced by the led group and the level of maturity or readiness (competence and motivation = knowing and welling) of each subordinate to manage different situations.

Understanding the phenomenon of cerebral multipolarity reinforces this thesis and enriches it, providing the leader with high-value instruments for diagnosing the various situations faced by the group and the level of maturity of each subordinate, as well as for adapting the behavior of the leader in the process communication with each subordinate.

Planner, controller, maker, driver, inspirer or creator. No matter what your dominant profile may be, your success as a leader will be determined by your ability to adjust your behavior to the specific situational needs of each of your subordinates.

Think: "This subordinate, in the present situation and task will perform better if I ...

describe the steps of the task and let all the execution in his hands?

describe the steps of the task and demand continuous information on the progress of performance?

Instead of describing the steps of the task, just deliver the task step by step?

Involve myself personally in the fulfillment of the task, helping the subordinate to perform it?

Paul Hershey and Kenneth Blanchard in the celebrated Situational Leadership text, gave a clear and logic movement the leader's behaviors, through the original Tannembaum & Schmidt dueling concept of "Follower Autonomy X Leader's Intervention:

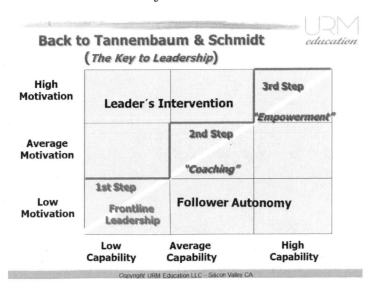

* * *

The importance of diverse Skills

What are the most important brain skills?
This is a question that tends to be answered in different ways by different people.

Those with dominant skills in either pole, satisfied and happy with the results they have achieved in life and at work, will tend to say that the most important skills are their favorites.

Others, dissatisfied with their performance, will tend to value the skills they would like to have, but do not have.

In general, most people will recognize that all skills are important in life and at work, depending on the circumstances that arise and the challenges posed by the environment.

In the early evolution of humanity, living in the forest or in the caves, the most brilliant intellectual with vigorous aptitudes in the left neocortical pole (NW), but with slow reflexes in his medullary pole (S), could be the tiger's first meal in the morning.

Likewise, the first athlete to reach the highest branch of the tree, fleeing from his pursuers, would be the first to plummet in the mathematics entrance exam when brought to the contemporary environment.

In the twentieth century environment, it is easy to see that all skills, and particularly their combinations, are fundamental to sustaining family, business and society life.

This occurs so sharply that research has shown that more than 70% of all marriages and unions, to constitute the first family, are celebrated between men and women of opposite brain dominance, which suggests a search, even if unconscious, for complementarity.

Likewise, when a company is constituted, people with specific (and specialized) brain dominance are allocated in different areas.

Over time, it appears that the difficulties in communication between representatives of such different universes of thought cause both the breakdown of symbiotic unions in the home and the friction and weariness of business efforts.

As we noted in the previous chapter, preventive/organizational was the dominant standard in business management until the 1960s, while today many companies tend to devalue these approaches to the benefit of more conceptual management.

But it is necessary to note that humanity owes a lot to the organizational (SW).

Under the inspiration of the conceptual, he started and provided, just over 7,000 years ago, agriculture and the domestication of animals (grazing), taking man out of his condition as a nomadic predator and slave of the environment for much more than 50,000 years.

The sequence of access and use of brain skills suggested in the entrepreneurial process show how the different skills are complementary to each other producing, as a whole, all the reasoning, studies and actions necessary for the creation, maintenance and progress of societies.

Integrity and balance, more than brightness or prominence in any of the skill poles, will maximize your potential for personal and professional fulfillment.
You have the right, the possibility and the duty to fully use all the skills with which nature toasted you. Do it.

* * *

25

Skills Development Exercises

Following a personal growth and development plan to increase your potential for achievement at work or in life requires, first of all, that you make a comparison between your dominant skills and those required by the position you occupy or aspire to.

Or the profession or destination you want to follow.

It is important for you to know that preference and competence are not the same. You can take much greater pleasure in poetic activities and still be very competent in mathematics because performance will also depend on your knowledge and experience.

You may not even like bureaucratic activities and perform them very well.

Deep down, you know that by doing what you love, you can be both competent and happy. Therefore, the development of your skills and dominance, alongside your knowledge and experience, will always be useful.

The self-help literature has placed great emphasis on the development of creative and communication skills, as if they, in isolation, were the "key" to success and happiness.

But that is not the truth.

Many people, in many professions, can benefit greatly from developing their creativity and communication skills (right hemisphere).

But it is also true that many excellent communicators and creative geniuses have already failed in their efforts and level of personal satisfaction due to lack of organization, discipline and rational self-criticism.

All skills are important and the need for their greater or lesser development and use depends on the goals and interests of each of us and the specific challenges we face.

In general, it is better to develop all of your skills to access and use flexibly, according to the situations that arise, in life and at work.

In addition, understanding and valuing the different skills maximizes your potential for coexistence and cooperation with everyone.

No man is an island. If you become aware of the uniqueness of your dominant skills and understand their value, while also becoming aware of the uniqueness of others 'skills, understanding their value in the same way, you will be capable of acting to make the difference between you and the others, instead of creating barriers of communication, complement each other and produce multiplied energy for you to work and live together.

You have certainly noticed that we all tend to judge others by their similarity to us.

They seem correct when they think like us or pray for our booklet, and even extremely wrong – unpleasant or stupid – if their attitudes and behaviors are much different from ours.

You don't have to be super smart to realize that the stranger or more objectionable a person seems to us, the more strange and objectionable we will appear to them.

This is just a fact of life. Each human being thinks with his own head. He makes decisions and takes action based on his own ideas.

The first step in the process of growing and mastering our brain skills is the ability to look and see the world and people from different perspectives of brain dominance, and then and as a consequence, the ability to communicate effectively with everyone.

"The root of altruism is empathy, the ability to read emotions in others... without a sense of the other's needs or despair there is no involvement".

All people have skills in all areas of brain dominance and, consequently, the possibility to develop these skills through appropriate exercises.

The levels of difficulty to do this depend, basically, on the relative breadth of the skills that are intended to develop and on the direction of the intended change.

The aspect of relative amplitude is obvious: if the person's skills are moderately developed at any pole, the basis for his development will be greater than the one found in the case of low skills.

The direction of change, however, implies specific inherent difficulties at eight different levels.

The lowest level of difficulty will be found by people with dominant skills at the NW or NE poles to develop their skills at the SW or SE poles, respectively (step down, in the same cerebral hemisphere).

The highest level of difficulty will be found by people with dominant skills at the SW pole (naturally more resistant to change) to develop skills at the NE pole (above and in the opposite cerebral hemisphere).

The adult brain dominance profile was mold by its genetic heritage and shaped by education and social interaction throughout its first years of life. We cannot change it at will, but we can manage it and place it under conscious control.

This scale of difficulties suggests a natural roadmap for the process of attack and development of non-dominant skills.

A person with dominant skills at the organizational pole and a low level of skills at the conceptual pole will have great difficulty in moving directly from that pole to the other. The exercises to do this, focused on the next chapter, while potentially effective, will be difficult (or unpleasant) for a person with such contrasting and sometimes antagonistic skills.

It will be easier to opt for a transition exercise script, going through difficulty level 2 so that, after exercising your skills in the factual pole, you can go to the typical exercises of the conceptual pole (difficulty level 4).

A similar journey can be undertaken by an individual with dominant skills at the factual pole who is committed to developing skills at the relational pole. It will be easier for him to descend to the organizational pole located in the same hemisphere (level of difficulty 1) and, from there, to start in parallel for the development of his relational skills (level of difficulty 4).

The exercises described below are specific to the development of the skills of each pole. They are classified into three categories of difficulty in this process, from lowest to highest.

1. Exercises to increase skills for environmental

reading and diagnosis of situations.

2. Exercises to adapt attitudes and behaviors to the demands of the environment.

3. Exercises to increase communication and negotiation skills.

1. Preventive/Organizational Pole (SW)

To develop the skills of observing the environment through the SW pole you have to look at the world and things in the same way as an individual whose dominant skills are located at that pole.

In general, try to observe, in all things, its shape, position and movement.

Also note the ordering or sequence between things or events and their parts.

Try to calculate the age of things and their temporal relationship, looking for answers to questions when, since when or until when.

Look at the details and observe the colors, lights and shadows. Try to calculate (not guess) the temperature of the observed objects.

Consider its usefulness or potential threat.

To train typical SW pole attitudes and behaviors, perform the following exercises from time to time:

- Make a family budget and check it periodically.
- Prepare a weekly activity plan and assemble a spreadsheet to control these activities.
- Make a complete inventory of your assets (and list).
- Organize your things (books, disks, tools, photographs) with some sort of sequential order and create an index.

- Systematically check your bank statements and cash receipts from the supermarket.
- Draw up a daily schedule of activities and stick to it.
- Plan and carry out a trip with all the activities previously determined and listed.
- Create files at home or in your office.
- Study a little bit of accounting and grammar.

To exercise your communication skills at this pole, which means learning to communicate effectively with dominantly preventive/organizational people, show everything that can be shown, using illustrations, photos, posters, charts and sequential tables, synoptic tables, etc.

- Use your body to convey ideas with specific movements to illustrate and "draw" your exhibition, avoiding physical proximity, useless or potentially threatening gestures.
- Use expressions typical of the SW's preferred vocabulary, such as: see, look well, stay tuned. Mention the organization, the sequence, the order, the discipline.
- Avoid expressions of relational vocabulary (SE) like trust, feel, go for me, I guarantee, get close, a hug and, mainly, of intuitive vocabulary (NE) like don't worry, calm, relaxed, listen, suppose, imagine, dare.
- Plan the sequence of the presentation and its arguments starting with the premises and reaching the consequent conclusions.
- Face your interlocutor during the interview. Ask him to explain and show things: show

me, let me see.

- Do not look away, do not get distracted, do not change the subject abruptly, do not constantly change your position and, above all, do not move away or withdraw before obtaining confirmation from your interlocutor that the matter is already concluded.

2. Emotional/Relational Pole (SE)

To develop the skills of observing the environment through the SE pole, you have to look at the world and things in the same way as an individual whose dominant skills are located at that pole.

- In general, try to observe people more than things and, in things, their relationship or similarity with living beings and people.
- Note the textures, harmony and plasticity or inherent poetry. Its sonority, expressiveness or beauty.
- Try to pay attention to people's feelings, needs and problems. And how people and things relate emotionally to you.
- Look at the environment in a romantic and affectionate way searching for bonds of affection with everything and everyone.

To train typical SE pole attitudes and behaviors, perform the following exercises from time to time:

- Greet people on the street.
- Thank everyone who serves you.

- Hug people and pet animals.
- Help others.
- Invite and gather friends.
- Go to parties and participate intensely.
- Tell stories to your children and friends.
- Play with your children (the way they want to play).
- Teach things you know.
- Listen to people carefully and praise.
- Listen to your music and dance while listening (keep pace).
- Read poetry and declare it out loud.
- Watch and enjoy movies of love and tenderness.

To exercise your communication skills at this pole, which means learning to communicate effectively with dominantly emotional/relational people, let go of your body and reveal your feelings.

- Explore your voice, rhythm, speed, timbre and modulation.
- Show feeling and enthusiasm. Follow and imitate your interlocutor's gestures.
- Approach your interlocutor and touch him.
- Listen a lot and encourage him to speak and gesture, expressing interest in his feelings and motivations.
- Do not walk away or be tense when he approaches you or imitates your gestures. Allow him to touch you.
- Use typical expressions of the SE's preferred vocabulary, such as: feel, trust, impressions, feelings.

- Avoid expressions typical of the organizational vocabulary (SW) as "see", "look", "be attentive", "careful" and, mainly, of the factual vocabulary (NW) as "examine", "analyze", "evaluate", "facts", "evidences".
- Try to know and write down, before any interview with an emotional/relational person, what your feelings, interests and beliefs are in order to be able to associate with those interests that may be common with yours and establish personal bonds during the conversation.
- "Empathy" is the name of the game. And "tunning", the name of the process.
- Nothing is so wrong as the popular quote -"If I were you..." (I'd do it differently). "If you were me... you'd do as I do".
- Every man thinks with his head. Makes decisions ad takes action upon his own ideas.
- Anybody can accept your ideas or visions but only after decide (with his own mind) to do that.

Exercising your non dominant skills does not guarantee that you will be better than the other.
But will surely guarantee that you will understand much better all the others.

And develop Empathy.

*The human brain
and the aptitudes it contains
can be strengthened by continuous exercise
in the same way as the muscles.
But, routinely, we only tend to exercise
our dominant skills.
To develop the capacity for the full use of
our brain skills we will have to exercise
our secondary skills as well.*

26

Access and use of non-dominant Skills

It will be easy to see that the execution of these exercises with some frequency and insistence, either by dedicating some time daily or, at least, weekly for this purpose, will contribute in a relevant way to the automatic development of your brain skills.

Science already knows that the brain, like muscles, is strengthened through exercise and you will have the opportunity to notice that these exercises will leave clear and immediate marks on your interests and abilities.

After a series of exercises for observing the environment through the organizational pole, for example, you will find that you begin to notice "shadows" that you normally did not notice in things.

We all notice, most of the time, the dark shadows cast by sunlight or artificial lighting, but we rarely see the small and tender shadows caused only by faint light or in dim environments (which predominantly organizational/ visual individuals have always noticed).

We will also see that our sensitivity to movements and textures can be greatly increased and, above all, that our imagination tends to become exacerbated right after the conceptual pole exercises, leaving indelible marks on our spirit.

It seems needless to say that the relational pole exercises will make us much more sympathetic and that they will lead other people to present themselves as much more sympathetic to us.

It has also been observed that many of these exercises are able to lead us to enjoy activities and positions that we simply did not admit or practice before, consequently and forever developing the breadth of our skills.

We will also have the opportunity to see that the quality of these skills will be enhanced, which, in other words, means that we can also become more intelligent.

And, of course, we will realize that our ability to communicate with anyone in any of the dominant skill poles will grow exponentially.

This will produce immediate and concrete results in improving our performance at work and in everyday life.

To find greater ease and enjoyment in performing these exercises it is important that you check and write down which are the easiest and most difficult exercises for you, numbering them in an hierarchical sequence (1, 2, 3, 4 etc.) and performing them always in that sequence.

This note is essential for you to meet the recommendations contained in the Appendix of this book, when we will address the exercises for multi dominance and access to closed poles.

Interested or not interested in developing the set of your brain skills, you can, with great advantage, make full use of the skills you have, whatever their level.

To do this, it is important that you address the situations you need to deal with or the problems you need to solve, in life or at work, in the following order:

1. Identify the events, situations, opportunities, threats or problems that will be the target of your attention and establish priorities for approach.

This provision is essential for you to effectively take charge of your destiny and not to waste all your time and all your energies simply reacting to the situations imposed on you by the environment, attacking them as they arise.

It is evident that no matter how much you orient yourself towards establishing your own priorities, adopting a proactive attitude (trying to anticipate events) at every opportunity, there will always be situation in which you will have to react to unexpected events.

However, the less you worry about predicting and planning for the future, the more unexpected all events will be and you will spend more time exhibiting frankly reactive attitudes and behaviors (always "chasing your tail").

2. Adapt all your attitudes, behaviors and available resources to the contingencies of each identified situation, trying to plan (think ahead) what to do to explore or keep these situations under control.

3. Effectively communicate your goals and proposals to achieve the adhesion, contribution and commitment of all the people around you, on whom the success of your projects depends, which means selling your ideas successfully.

The process of identifying and understanding the situations around you, in order to meet the measures suggested in item 1, uses, fundamentally, the characteristic abilities of the intuitive (NE) and rational (NW) poles and can be enriched by asking questions that aim to:

1. Qualify situations (what?)
2. Clear them (how?)
3. Locate them in space (where?)
4. Locate them in time (when?)
5. Quantify them (how much?)
6. Identify their agents (who?)
7. Find their causes (why?)

These seven questions: what, how, where, when, how much, who and why make up the basic heuristic developed by the Greek philosopher Aristotle, in classical antiquity, when humanity had much less knowledge than today and needed to ask more.

They are often forgotten in a civilization like ours where it seems to many of us that everything is already known and that there is nothing more to be asked.

However, if you always and systematically ask these questions in the face of all the situations you have to deal with, you will quickly realize how much you lack and need to know so that you can better guide your actions.

To establish priorities for your actions and goals, after listing chosen situations around you, submit each of these situations to the following questions:

- What is or will be the impact of this situation

or problem on my global goals and interests (or on the results of my work)?

- What is the "manageability" (ease of handling) of this situation or problem?

You will see, through these questions, that many situations that afflict you have, in reality, very little impact on your life and work, in such a way that you can simply stop worrying about them or, at least, not spending too much time with them, to be able to devote most of your attention, efforts and priorities to addressing the situations with the greatest impact in your life.

You will also see that many situations of significant impact on your life have very low manageability, that is: you practically have no way to solve them, resulting in your approach being a waste of time and effort. Has anyone ever said to sum up this concept: "If your problems have a solution, why bother? If they have no solution, why bother?

The cartoon The Lion King released the chorus "Hakuna matata" to say the same thing.

Evidently, the proposal is not for you to throw everything in the air, but to use your rational skills in order to determine what are, in reality, the priorities in your life and work.

In business language, this has been treated as the process of choosing critical business success factors or different actions within the business.

Critical success factors are those few things that we need to treat with care and do well to ensure most of our results. They exist both at work and in each person's daily life.

Once you have chosen your priorities, whether in

life, at work or in managing the work of others, you need to put these priorities in the typical language for each of the skill poles, which corresponds to putting your skill set at the service of your goals, as well as creating conditions for the involvement in your goals and projects of people with different dominances of brain aptitudes.

Here's how it works in practice.

The intuitive pole (NE) visualizes the responses that depend on synthesis, imagination, intuition, and gathers the responses generated in the other poles in a whole that makes sense.

The factual pole (NW) deduces the responses that depend on data collection and analysis, evaluates and provides factual anchors to the responses generated intuitively (NE) and sensitively (SE).

The organizational pole (SW) provides the responses that imply functionality and protection to the action plans, organizes and prints a logical sequence to the responses coming from the other poles.

The relational pole (SE) helps others with responses capable of involving and sensitizing people and provides emotional anchors (affective commitment) for responses from all other poles.

In short, the full use of all brain skills in life, work and management comes down to a question of not allowing your dominant skills to take over the whole picture.

Whenever you are dealing with a problem or situation, you will tend to use your dominant skills, exclusively or first of all.

Be aware of this reality and the dangers it represents and do not allow it to happen.

Spiritual Phenomena

The illustrative model of the distribution of brain aptitudes has two central nuclei: the medullary pole (S) and the post-cortical pole (N).

The medullary pole, seat of unconscious and subconscious bodily / visceral aptitudes, is the oldest portion of the central nervous system, repository of the entire ancestral heritage of man.

In this pole, as must be evident, man has bonds with all his ancestors.

You have inherited many skills from your parents. They from their grandparents. The grandparents from the great-grandparents and so on.

You can imagine, although you might not have thought of it before, that your brain holds, within itself, some inheritance from the Teriodontis with whom we started our journey.

You may be a direct descendant of a happy couple of them.

The post-cortical pole, home of the metaphysical / spiritual, supra-intellectual and supraconscious aptitudes, is the newest and most noble (and in an accelerated development) portion of the human brain capable of carrying out ultra-sophisticated combinations of knowledge and imagination.

There you have a bond with your descendants, with the man of the future and with the demigod with quasi-Divine powers (QuaD).

These two poles appear visually as the central axis of the brain, as its nucleus or, in other words, as the "soul" of that structure.

We developed this metaphorical view intentionally to suggest that these two poles, linked together in the center of the brain, effectively constitute the soul of the human being.

This is exactly what you just read: the soul, as we have always defined and understood it, is the essence of the human spirit summarized at the extremities of our aptitudes: to know and to act.

Let's explain this better.

The scientific evidence compiled until today does not allow to affirm, although the same cannot be categorically denied, that the information stored in memory can be transmitted genetically and, consequently, received hereditarily.

Archetypes – patterns of seemingly innate attitudes and behaviors – are seen by many as powerful indicators that learned concepts can be passed on hereditarily.

But it is not necessary to admit the transmission of knowledge through the genes to understand that memories stored by parents are transmitted to their children on the margins of educational processes.

There are at least two other channels to guarantee this effect.

First, intrauterine coexistence: for nine months the fetuses shared much more with their mothers than blood, oxygen and other chemical agents. As an integral part of the maternal organism during this period, with a nervous system and a brain already in development, the fetus received from the mother all the chemical and electrical impulses that passed through the mother's nervous system and, therefore, all the sensory information contained therein. It is not heresy to say that the child, at birth, has in its brain all the information that was in the mother's brain.

In addition, before and after birth, we receive a great deal of information from our parents and everyone around us through known sensory pathways – it has long been known that fetuses hear and can react to information received through the auditory pathway, and store them by extra-sensorial ways – sensitive systems not yet clearly cataloged, but almost obvious.

We have no reason to doubt that the human mind can receive and send messages telepathically as through radio waves in space. Devices much simpler than the human brain – rudimentary, by the way, when compared to it – do this every day.

Thus, it is possible to understand that we have in our mind a large amount of information received unconsciously from many people and most, if not all, of the information accumulated in the minds of our parents and, by reasoning, of all our ancestors.

Carl Jung, the Swiss psychologist, who at the beginning of the century was Freud's disciple, developed the concept of the collective unconscious in the following decade: a reservoir where the memories of the past of all humanity would be stored – as if it were a bank of souls.

With that possibility in mind, we can conceive an immortal soul regardless of any religious beliefs.

By associating the ideas of the soul and information contained in the brain and the logic of the inheritance of ancestral information, it is easy to see that the soul in the sense proposed here will, in fact, be immortal, eternalizing itself in the transition from parents to children and other recipients of memories ancestors (Figure A.1).

From this reasoning point of view, many spiritual phenomena, including and particularly those related to memories of past lives, would be explainable not through the belief in reincarnations of the spirit, but simply through the transmission of memories from one generation to another, in direct line or through triangulations.

If and when anyone brings back memories of past lives, he may know that the events seen or felt did not occur with himself in other incarnations, but with his

grandparents, great-grandparents or any other more distant ancestors or with people with whom they lived.

Thinking carefully and understanding as "soul" the people's unconscious and the information accumulated therein, we will arrive exactly at the idea of reincarnation proposed by spiritualists free of mystical or religious connotations, such as virtues or sins, guilt and punishment imposed by divinity or destiny.

It is even simpler to imagine how the concept of the soul and the unconscious can explain the contact with people who no longer live or with the reception of messages from these people.

As all people continue to "live" in their descendants, the information that emerges in these meetings or in the messages received can have its origin in the soul of a living person, present or not in the opportunity, where they would be filed at subconscious or unconscious levels.

Science already knows that 99% of all information received by humans through known sensory receptors is discarded by the brain as being irrelevant and unimportant (requiring no response).

We also know that all information not used for the generation of responses will be filed for future use in motor or intellectual activities.

In fact, the amount of information and experience we have accumulated at the subconscious and unconscious levels is infinitely greater than that passing through the conscious at any time.

Just think about it a little to realize how many experiences we can relive personally or through third parties to whom we pass telepathically information contained in our unconscious. And also, how many experiences can we live by receiving telepathic information from others.

Telepathy is, in fact, an ability that is seen as trivial by many people, although it is evident that we cannot exercise it as we please. There are numerous reports of experiences of transmission of thoughts lived by many individuals who never considered themselves to have any special telepathic or mediumistic "gift".

In the fields of parapsychology, it is taken for granted that the potential of the human mind or spirit far exceeds the skills that we move about in our daily lives.

This potentiality cannot be accessed directly and in a programmed way, but, through the exercises proposed for the development of brain skills and all systems of representation, it will be greatly strengthened.

Hypothesis for the Future
Extracted from the combination of knowledge and imagination

N

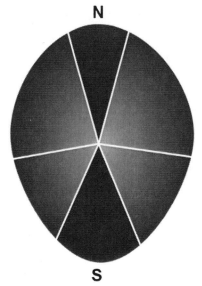

S

Memories of past lives
Acquired in intrauterine coexistence and in extrasensory communication

SPIRITUAL INTELLIGENCE

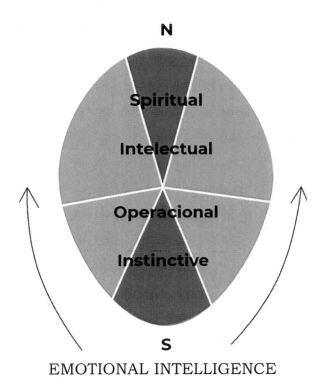

EMOTIONAL INTELLIGENCE

Figure A.1 The long, long journey from instincts to QuaD

* * *

Intellectual control of Emotions and vice versa

While the cerebral cortex interferes with the operation of the lower brain centers, providing precision and refinement to the body's movements, the lower brain centers agitate the cerebral cortex, keeping it in alert for the production of information essential to understanding the environment and formulation of decisions to optimize the actions to be adopted.

The knowledge of this essential interrelationship and inter cooperation between the operating and intellectual systems allows us to use our bodies to influence our minds as much as our minds to influence our bodies.

We have all had the opportunity to get rid of tension states simply by relaxing the body, sitting or lying down and breathing slowly (pretending to be calm).

We can, in the same way, go the other direction.

We can assume a state of great agitation and even anger if we pretend to be angry. Our pulse will rise, our breathing will be truncated and we will be in a crescendo of real nervousness and legitimate anger.

This phenomenon stems from the fact that spontaneous and sudden movements (without refinement) dispense the interference of neocortical (intellectual) mechanisms, leaving us under de commandment of the emotional brain.

In classical ballet, we have a typical example of very refined movements, commanded by the neocortex. The ballet performed by the trained puppy can be very graceful, but it will always be punctuated by discontinuous movements.

The emotional brain, we know, is not just angry. It is also tender and romantic, cheerful, sad or whining.

This characteristic can also be exploited to reduce the interference of neocortical mechanisms in our actions.

Pretending that we are sad, assuming sad thoughts and trying hard to be moved and cry, we will, very often, be moved and really cry.

In his book Emotional Intelligence, Goleman referred to this capacity in the actors: to pretend feelings and, therefore, to really assume those feelings.

Any of us can do this, with some persistence and training.

It is clearly evident that, through the use of music, we can both calm down and excite ourselves. What happens in practice is that music can invoke states of great calm and emotional relaxation, as well as vigorous feelings and emotions accessing neocortical (intellectual) circuits or emotional circuits.

The fact is that we can do both without the external help of music, using only our mind and body to reproduce the same effects.

A very revealing experience in this sense is the use of smooth, controlled and complex movements, such as, for example, the simultaneous movement, in slow motion, of the joints of the shoulders, elbows, wrists, hands and fingers in different directions and amplitudes, accompanied by paused breathing.

You will find that you are making a type of movement that no other animal would ever manage to do. These movements are commanded by the neocortex and require continuous monitoring.

Whenever you are very angry, almost out of your mind, you will quickly recover your calm and the control of your emotions simply by repeating these movements.

More than that, you will find that the more carefully you move, the faster you will control your anger.

Domain of the Body

The increase in limbic energy and the speed of reaction to stimuli in the environment will be easier for individuals with dominant skills at the cortical poles (SW and SE) than neocortical ones (NW and NE).

Anyone who met people with high emotional energy knows how they can move from calm to fury in a fraction of a second.

Downward movements are easier to reproduce because they take us to much more experienced areas of the brain, which we used intensively at some point in our evolution (Figure B.1).

Voluntarily or involuntarily, we can increase our load of emotion and our visceral reactions in response to physical or psychic excitement: getting into a traffic fight, arguing with exasperated colleagues, recalling unpleasant experiences, self imposing physical pain, just raising your voice.

But this movement alone will not guarantee a deep dive into the instinctual pole. We will not be able, even in a state of exacerbated tension, to control our unconscious or subconscious organic activities, nor to rescue, as we please, memories stored at these levels (ancestral memories).

This movement will only be possible as we progressively manage to discard, one by one, the cortical and neocortical (conscious) reasonings and concerns that populate our mind and occupy it all the time.

If we manage not to think or plan, to erase conscious human involvement from the mind, to forget control, to sublimate discipline, to eliminate the present bonds with the environment and with people until reaching a stage of aptitudes and interests reduced to the capacities of action, reaction and scape, typical of the lower animals on the zoological scale, we will be almost automatically immersed in our visceral pole.

It is very unlikely that we will be able to do this without eliminating the external interference typical of a sophisticated environment such as urban, for example.

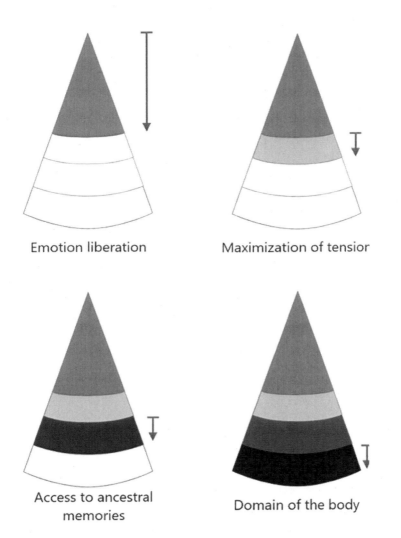

Emotion liberation

Maximization of tensior

Access to ancestral
memories

Domain of the body

Figure B.1 Rescue of limbic aptitudes

In conditions of total isolation or internment in environments free from the interference of modern technology products: electric light, vehicles, radio or TV, for example, the only intervening variable that we have to control would be our own thoughts.

If, on the other hand, like what happens in states of deep hypnosis or complete drunkenness, managing to completely abstract the external intervening factors, it is quite possible that we will be able, if not to assume the unconscious or subconscious organic movements, to recover some accumulated memories in the medullary levels (ancestral memories or memories of past lives).

Even providing favorable environmental conditions, any attempts to access the skills and memories of the spinal pole will not produce results more than incidentally, hindering, if not making impossible, the conscious and controlled reproduction of the process.

This access, to prevent frustrations, can be attempted by concentrating efforts on typical exercises for the development of SW and SE skills, with a progressive departure from neocortical skills, that is, performing the exercises proposed on a descending scale:

1. Exercises difficulty 4

2. Exercises difficulty 3

3. Exercises difficulty 2

and so on, depending on the notes you have made.

This means that we will try to access this closed pole step by step, starting with a process of releasing emotions to maximize tension and only then drifting towards possible access to ancestral memories pursuing the full domain of the body.

A curious illustration of this process has been popularized through the fictional hero The Incredible Hulk, in comics and on the television series.

In the stories of the Hulk, Dr. Banner, a scientist

and intellectual, assumed, in states of psychic exasperation (under great suffering or pain), an extraordinary physical force, the ferocity and intellectual obtuseness of the caveman.

It is curious to note that the character quickly moved from a neocortical (intellectual) stage to a pre-cortical and medullary (limbic/visceral) stage, while remaining, nevertheless, affectionate and romantic with the children and with other "friendly" animals. In fact, the focused character has exactly the skills described in the first stage of evolution.

We mention this example specifically to create an opportunity to say that what we call maximizing tension is not going into a state of fury or anger, but simply breaking free from intellectual anchors and conscious reasoning to dive deep into the subconscious and unconscious levels of mind.

This, in most cases, will occur in states of full relaxation.

Thus, and for that reason, relaxation and self-hypnosis exercises can be extraordinarily functional in this process, but they, unless incidentally, will not produce results if they are not preceded by the conscious exercises proposed here.

Domain of the Spirit

In the same way as the one proposed for the rescue of visceral or medullary aptitudes, and with much greater certainty, the broad domain of spiritual aptitudes will prove to be an extremely complex experiment.

We will not approach any mystical formula for doing this because, quite generally, people who have had spiritual experiences of some depth cannot explain why or how they came to be.

Those that propose to explain the process end up suggesting magic formulas whose controlled effect could never be demonstrated.

It seems beyond doubt that some people have greater aptitudes than others to access spiritual powers and it is possible that many of us will never be able to do so.

However, the proposal raised in this book that quasi-divine aptitudes constitute a kind of summation or depletion of all other human aptitudes suggests a rational way to encourage the development of these aptitudes.

Through the exercises proposed to achieve what we are calling multi dominance – an attempt to sequentially develop all brain skills in the same order in which they appear and use – we will, as if exhausting cortical and neocortical skills, be ready to enter the field reserved for post-cortical aptitudes.

The sequence of exercises suggested for this purpose begins with the series aimed at the development of organizational (SW) and relational (SE) skills, deriving in continuity for the series aimed at the development of factual (NW) and conceptual (NE) skills, always in an order of difficulty and increasing complexity (1, 2, 3, 4...), according to the notes you made in the exercises starting on page 152.

This sequence, which we call pressure for multi-dominance, aims to explore all the skills known by the brain towards the domain of QuaD skills (Figure B.2).

It starts with the sublimation of emotions

(leaving the limbic system) towards the purification of the intellect (wide domain of neocortical skills) before accessing QuaD skills and successive effort to master the spirit.

In this process, it is important to remember that, although opposed in their position, functions and development hierarchy over millennia, the medullary and post-cortical poles are closely linked in their extrasensory capacities.

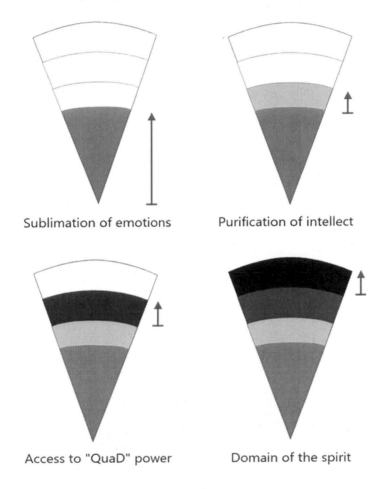

Sublimation of emotions   Purification of intellect

Access to "QuaD" power   Domain of the spirit

Figure B.2 QuaD skills development

In fact, they are linked together physically and sensorially assembling the group that we dare to call the soul of the system.

Our QuaD capacities, as well as the visceral ones, are manifested sub and unconsciously (in this case, supra consciously) in such a way that the ancestral memories contained in our brain can lend a very significant reinforcement to their access.

For this reason, relaxation, hypnosis and self-hypnosis exercises can also be important assistants in this process, as long as, in the same way, preceded by exhaustive dedication to perform the conscious exercises that were proposed in the multi-dominance sequence.

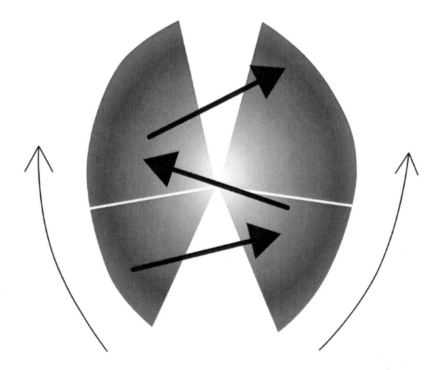

Figure B. 2 Pressure towards multi-dominance.

- *GO TOTAL BRAIN!*

*Exercise the development
of your talents
following the same sequency
through which nature and evolution
molded them.
Step by step, beginning with the rescue
and reinforcement of your Corporal Talents
to Organizational Talents,
then Social Talents, Critical, Creative
and Spiritual Talents.
The idea is to access, occupy and optimize
the exploration of each of the six brains
inside your brain, to create pressure
towards the enrichment of your
Spiritual Intelligence.*